RENEWED BY
THE MOST HOLY SECOND ECUMENI
PROMULGATED BY AUTHC
AND REVISED AT THE DIRECTI

GENERAL INSTRUCTION OF THE ROMAN MISSAL

AND UNIVERSAL NORMS FOR THE LITURGICAL YEAR AND THE GENERAL ROMAN CALENDAR

MMX

Catholic Bishops' Conference
of England and Wales

The Bishops' Conference
of Scotland

CATHOLIC TRUTH SOCIETY
PUBLISHERS TO THE HOLY SEE

Published by
THE CATHOLIC TRUTH SOCIETY
40-46 Harleyford Road, London, SE11 5AY

General Instruction of the Roman Missal: ISBN 978 1 86082 812 6
CTS Code RM12

CONTENTS

GENERAL INSTRUCTION OF THE ROMAN MISSAL

INTRODUCTION

CHAPTER I

THE IMPORTANCE AND DIGNITY

CHAPTER II

CHAPTER V
THE ARRANGEMENT AND ORNAMENTATION OF CHURCHES

CHAPTER VI

CHAPTER VII

CHAPTER VIII

CHAPTER IX

UNIVERSAL NORMS FOR THE LITURGICAL YEAR AND THE GENERAL ROMAN CALENDAR

CONGREGATION FOR DIVINE WORSHIP
AND DISCIPLINE OF THE SACRAMENTS

Prot. N. 143/00/L

DECREE
CONCERNING THE THIRD TYPICAL EDITION

At the outset of the third millennium after the Incarnation of the Lord, it has been decided to prepare a new edition of the *Missale Romanum*, to take account of the more recent documents of the Apostolic See and especially of the new Code of Canon Law, and to meet the various needs for emendation and augmentation.

Regarding the *Institutio Generalis Missalis Romani*, some variations have been introduced consistent with the manner of expression and prescriptions of other liturgical books and also recommended by pastoral experience. The permitted cases regarding the faculty to distribute Holy Communion under both kinds are set out more clearly; a newly-composed Chapter 9 has been added, in which a way is outlined of adapting the Roman Missal in an appropriate way to pastoral needs.

Other formulas have been added for celebrations recently inserted into the General Roman Calendar. With the aim of fostering devotion to the Mother of God, the Common of the Blessed Virgin Mary has been endowed with new Mass formularies. Likewise, in other Commons, in Masses for Various Needs and Occasions and in the Masses for the Dead, the order of prayers has from time to time been changed for the sake of greater consistency in the texts. In the Masses of Lent, in accord with ancient liturgical practice, a Prayer over the People has been inserted for each day.

In an appendix to the Order of Mass are also to be found the Eucharistic Prayer for Reconciliation and a special Eucharistic Prayer, which may be used for various needs.

9

The Supreme Pontiff John Paul II approved by his authority this third edition of the Roman Missal on 10 April 2000, and the Congregation for Divine Worship and Discipline of the Sacraments now publishes it and declares it to be typical.

Conferences of Bishops shall ensure that, within an appropriate period of time, new vernacular versions of the *Missale Romanum* are faithfully and accurately prepared from this third typical edition for the *recognitio* of the Apostolic See in accordance with the norm of law, with the preceding versions in use up till now being emended accurately in fidelity to the original Latin text.

Furthermore, this third typical Latin edition of the *Missale Romanum* may be used in the celebration of the Most Holy Eucharist from the day on which it is published, but it will come into force on the Solemnity of the Body and Blood of the Lord in the year 2000.

All things to the contrary notwithstanding.

From the offices of the Congregation for Divine Worship and Discipline of the Sacraments, 20 April, Thursday of the Lord's Supper, in the year of the Great Jubilee 2000.

JORGE A. Card. MEDINA ESTÉVEZ
Prefect

✠ FRANCESCO PIO TAMBURRINO
Archbishop Secretary

APOSTOLIC CONSTITUTION
MISSALE ROMANUM

APOSTOLIC CONSTITUTION

PROMULGATION OF THE *MISSALE ROMANUM* RENEWED BY DECREE OF THE SECOND ECUMENICAL COUNCIL OF THE VATICAN

PAUL, BISHOP

SERVANT OF THE SERVANTS OF GOD
FOR AN EVERLASTING MEMORIAL

The Missale Romanum, promulgated in accordance with the decree of the Council of Trent by Our Predecessor Saint Pius V in the year 1570,[1] is recognized by all as being numbered among the many wonderful fruits that issued from that same Sacred Synod to the benefit of the whole Church of Christ. For throughout four centuries not only have Priests of the Latin Rite had it as their norm for celebrating the Eucharistic Sacrifice, but messengers of the holy Gospel have also carried it into almost every land. Moreover, innumerable men of great holiness have abundantly nourished their devotion to God by drawing from it both readings taken from the Sacred Scripture and prayers, the chief part of which Saint Gregory the Great had arranged in a certain order.

Yet since the time when there began to grow and gain strength among the Christian people a concern for promoting the Sacred Liturgy which, in the opinion of Our Predecessor of venerable memory Pius XII, manifested both an indication of the very great favour of God's providence towards the men of this age, and the salvific movement of the Holy Spirit through his Church, it has similarly become clear that the formulas of

---

[1] Cf. Apostolic Constitution, *Quo primum*, 14 July 1570.

the Roman Missal need both to be somewhat revised and also to be enriched with additions.[2] This task Our same Predecessor inaugurated with the restoration of the Easter Vigil and of the Rite of Holy Week,[3] and thus took, as it were, a first step towards the adaptation of the Roman Missal to the sensitivities of this new age.

The recent Second Ecumenical Council of the Vatican, in the Constitution *Sacrosanctum Concilium*, laid the foundations for the general renewal of the Roman Missal, laying down that "texts and rites should be ordered in such a way that they express more clearly the holy things they signify,"[4] and later that "the Order of Mass should be revised in such a way that the purpose proper to its individual parts, as also the connection between them, may be more clearly evident, and that devout and active participation by the faithful may be facilitated,"[5] then that "the treasures of the Bible be opened up more abundantly so that richer fare may be spread before the faithful at the table of God's Word,"[6] and finally that "a new rite for concelebration is to be drawn up and inserted into the Roman Pontifical and the Roman Missal."[7]

However, it should in no way be thought that this revision of the Roman Missal has been introduced without preparation, since without any doubt the way was prepared by progress in liturgical disciplines these last four centuries. For if, after the Council of Trent, the reading and examination of "ancient manuscripts, both those in the Vatican library and others discovered elsewhere" helped not a little in the revision of the

---

[2]   Cf. Pius XII, *Discourse to the Participants in the First International Congress of Pastoral Liturgy at Assisi*, 22 September 1956: *Acta Apostolicae Sedis* 48 (1956), p. 712.

[3]   Cf. Sacred Congregation of Rites, Decree, *Dominicae Resurrectionis*, 9 February 1951: *Acta Apostolicae Sedis* 43 (1951), pp. 128ff.; General Decree, *Maxima redemptionis nostrae mysteria*, 16 November 1955: *Acta Apostolicae Sedis* 47 (1955), pp. 838ff.

[4]   Second Vatican Council, Constitution on the Sacred Liturgy, *Sacrosanctum Concilium*, no. 51.

[5]   Cf. *ibidem*, no. 50.

[6]   Cf. *ibidem*, no. 51.

[7]   Cf. *ibidem*, no. 58.

Roman Missal, as is confirmed by the Apostolic Constitution *Quo primum* issued by Our Predecessor Saint Pius V, subsequently on the one hand very ancient liturgical sources have of course been discovered and published, and on the other hand the liturgical formularies of the Eastern Church have been studied more deeply. As a result, it has been the desire of many that not only these doctrinal and spiritual riches not lie in the darkness of archives, but rather be brought out into the light to enlighten and nourish the minds and spirits of Christians.

Now, however, in order to set out, at least in broad outline, the new arrangement of the Roman Missal, We first point out that in the *Institutio Generalis*, which We have used as a proemium to the book, new norms are given for the celebration of the Eucharistic Sacrifice, regarding both the rites to be carried out and the functions proper to each person present and participating and to the furnishings and the places necessary for the conduct of divine worship.

The principal innovation is to be considered to lie in the restoration concerning the Eucharistic Prayer, as it is called. For although in the Roman Rite the first part of this Prayer, that is, the Preface, acquired various formulas over the passage of centuries, the second part, which was called the *Canon Actionis*, took on a fixed form between the fourth and fifth centuries; whereas, by contrast, the Oriental Liturgies admitted a certain variety among the Anaphoras themselves. Regarding this matter, besides the endowment of the Eucharistic Prayer with a number of Prefaces, either taken from the earlier tradition of the Roman Church or now newly composed, so that through them particular parts of the mystery of salvation may become more clearly evident and more numerous and richer motives for thanksgiving, We have also ordered that three new Canons be provided, added alongside this same Prayer. However, both for what are called pastoral reasons and to facilitate concelebration, We have ordered that the words of the Lord be one and the same in each formula of the Canon. Hence in each Eucharistic Prayer We wish those words to be proclaimed as follows: over the bread, *Accipite et manducate ex hoc omnes: Hoc est enim Corpus meum, quod pro vobis tradetur*; and over the chalice: *Accipite et bibite ex eo*

15

omnes: Hic est enim calix Sanguinis mei novi et aeterni testamenti, qui pro vobis et pro multis effundetur in remissionem peccatorum. Hoc facite in meam commemorationem. As to the words *Mysterium fidei*, removed from the context of the words of Christ our Lord and spoken by the Priest, these open the way, as it were, to the acclamation of the faithful.

Regarding the Order of Mass, "the rites have been simplified, due care being taken to preserve their substance."[8] For those things "that, with the passage of time, came to be duplicated or were added to little advantage"[9] have been omitted, especially with regard to the rites for the offering of the bread and wine and with regard to the rites of the breaking of the bread and of Communion.

Furthermore, "there have been restored ... in accordance with the ancient norm of the holy Fathers, various elements which have suffered injury through accidents of history."[10] Among such are the Homily,[11] the Universal Prayer or Prayer of the Faithful,[12] and the Penitential Rite or rite of reconciliation with God and with the brethren, to be enacted at the beginning of Mass: to which due importance has been restored, as was opportune.

In addition, according to the prescription of the Second Vatican Council that "over the course of a prescribed number of years a more representative portion of the Holy Scriptures be read to the people,"[13] the entire body of readings to be read on Sundays has been arranged over three years. Moreover, on days that are in any way festive, the readings of the Epistle and Gospel are preceded by another reading taken from the Old Testament, or during Easter Time from the Acts of the Apostles. For by this means, the continuous process of the mystery of salvation is illustrated, as set forth in the revealed words of God. This great

---

[8]   Cf. *ibidem*, no. 50.

[9]   Cf. *ibidem*, no. 50.

[10]   Cf. *ibidem*, no. 50.

[11]   Cf. *ibidem*, no. 52.

[12]   Cf. *ibidem*, no. 53.

[13]   Cf. *ibidem*, no. 51.

abundance of biblical readings, which sets before the faithful on feast days the most precious part of the Sacred Scriptures, is completed by the addition of other parts of the sacred books, which are read on days that are not festive.

All these things have been arranged in this way so as to arouse more and more among Christ's faithful that hunger for the Word of God[14] by which, under the guidance of the Holy Spirit, the people of the New Covenant can be seen, as it were, to be impelled towards the perfect unity of the Church. We trust that given this arrangement both Priests and faithful may make more devout spiritual preparation for the Lord's Supper and that, meditating more deeply on Sacred Scripture, they will be nourished more abundantly each day by the words of the Lord. In consequence, in accord with the teachings of the Second Vatican Council, Sacred Scripture will be regarded by all as an abiding fountain of spiritual life, as the principal basis for the handing on of Christian doctrine, and finally as the core of all theological formation.

In this restoration of the *Missale Romanum*, not only have the three parts We have already mentioned been changed, namely the Eucharistic Prayer, the Order of Mass, and the Order of Readings, but the others in which it consists have been revised and notably modified, that is: the Temporal, the Sanctoral, the Common of Saints, the Ritual Masses, and the Votive Masses, as they are called. Among these, particular care has been taken with the orations, which have not only been increased in number, so that new prayers respond to the new needs of these times, but also the most ancient prayers have been revised to accord with the ancient texts. As a result, to each weekday of the principal liturgical times, namely, Advent, Christmas, Lent, and Easter, has now been assigned its own distinct oration.

Moreover, although the text of the *Graduale Romanum*, at least as regards the music, has been left unchanged, for the sake of easier understanding, the Responsorial Psalm, which Saint Augustine and Saint Leo the Great often mention, and the

---

[14] Cf. *Amos* 8:11.

Entrance and Communion Antiphons for use where appropriate in Masses without singing, have been restored.

Finally, from the matters that We have explained so far concerning the new *Missale Romanum*, there is something that We are now pleased to insist upon and to effect. When Our Predecessor Saint Pius V promulgated the *editio princeps* of the *Missale Romanum*, he presented it to the Christian people as an instrument, as it were, of liturgical unity and as a monument of true and reverent worship in the Church. We, too, no less, even though We have accepted into the new Roman Missal "lawful variations and adaptations"[15] in virtue of what the Second Vatican Council prescribed, We are no less confident that it will be received by the Christian faithful as a help in witnessing to and strengthening the unity of all, by means of which, in the variety of so many languages, one and the same prayer of all will rise up, more fragrant than any incense, to the heavenly Father, through our High Priest Jesus Christ, in the Holy Spirit.

What We have prescribed in this Our Constitution shall enter into force on the thirtieth day of the month of November this year, that is, the First Sunday of Advent.

We decree that these Our laws and prescriptions be firm and effective now and in the future, notwithstanding, to the extent necessary, the Apostolic Constitutions and Ordinances issued by Our Predecessors nor other prescriptions, even those worthy of particular mention and derogation.

Given at Rome, at Saint Peter's, on the third day of the month of April, the day of the Supper of Our Lord Jesus Christ, in the year 1969, the sixth of Our Pontificate.

PAUL VI, POPE

---

[15] Cf. Second Vatican Council, Constitution on the Sacred Liturgy, *Sacrosanctum Concilium*, nos. 38-40.

GENERAL INSTRUCTION OF THE ROMAN MISSAL

INTRODUCTION

1.   As Christ the Lord was about to celebrate with the disciples the paschal supper in which he instituted the Sacrifice of his Body and Blood, he commanded that a large, furnished upper room be prepared (*Lk* 22:12). Indeed, the Church has always judged that this command also applied to herself whenever she decided about things related to the disposition of people's minds, and of places, rites and texts for the Celebration of the Most Holy Eucharist. The present norms, too, prescribed in keeping with the will of the Second Vatican Council, together with the new Missal with which the Church of the Roman Rite will henceforth celebrate the Mass, are again a demonstration of this same solicitude of the Church, of her faith and her unaltered love for the supreme mystery of the Eucharist, and also attest to her continuous and consistent tradition, even though certain new elements have been introduced.

Testimony of an Unaltered Faith

2.   The sacrificial nature of the Mass, solemnly defended by the Council of Trent, because it accords with the universal tradition of the Church,[1] was once more stated by the Second Vatican Council, which pronounced these clear words about the Mass: 'At the Last Supper, Our Saviour instituted the Eucharistic Sacrifice of his Body and Blood, by which the Sacrifice of his Cross is perpetuated until he comes again; and till then he entrusts the memorial of his Death and Resurrection to his beloved spouse, the Church'.[2]

What is taught in this way by the Council is consistently expressed in the formulas of the Mass. Moreover, the doctrine which stands out in the following sentence, already notable and

---

[1]   Ecumenical Council of Trent, Session XXII, 17 September 1562: Denzinger-Schönmetzer, nos. 1738-1759.

[2]   Second Ecumenical Council of the Vatican, Constitution on the Sacred Liturgy, *Sacrosanctum Concilium*, no. 47; cf. Dogmatic Constitution on the Church, *Lumen gentium*, nos. 3, 28; Decree on the Ministry and Life of Priests, *Presbyterorum ordinis*, nos. 2, 4, 5.

concisely expressed in the ancient Sacramentary commonly called the Leonine – 'for whenever the memorial of this sacrifice is celebrated the work of our redemption is accomplished'[3] – is aptly and exactly expounded in the Eucharistic Prayers; for as in these the Priest enacts the anamnesis, while turned towards God likewise in the name of all the people, he renders thanks and offers the living and holy sacrifice, that is, the Church's oblation and the sacrificial Victim by whose death God himself willed to reconcile us to himself;[4] and the Priest also prays that the Body and Blood of Christ may be a sacrifice which is acceptable to the Father and which brings salvation to the whole world.[5]

So, in the new Missal the rule of prayer (*lex orandi*) of the Church corresponds to her perennial rule of faith (*lex credendi*), by which we are truly taught that the sacrifice of his Cross and its sacramental renewal in the Mass, which Christ the Lord instituted at the Last Supper and commanded his Apostles to do in his memory, are one and the same, differing only in the manner of their offering; and as a result, that the Mass is at one and the same time a sacrifice of praise, thanksgiving, propitiation and satisfaction.

3.   Moreover, the wondrous mystery of the real presence of the Lord under the Eucharistic species, confirmed by the Second Vatican Council[6] and other teachings of the Church's Magisterium[7] in the same sense and with the same doctrine

---

[3]   Evening Mass of the Lord's Supper, Prayer over the Offerings. Cf. *Sacramentarium Veronense*, L.C. Mohlberg, editor, no. 93.

[4]   Cf. Eucharistic Prayer III.

[5]   Cf. Eucharistic Prayer IV.

[6]   Second Ecumenical Council of the Vatican, Constitution on the Sacred Liturgy, *Sacrosanctum Concilium*, nos. 7, 47; Decree on the Ministry and Life of Priests, *Presbyterorum ordinis*, nos. 5, 18.

[7]   Cf. Pius XII, Encyclical Letter, *Humani generis*, 12 August 1950: *Acta Apostolicae Sedis* 42 (1950), pp. 570-571; Paul VI, Encyclical Letter, *Mysterium fidei*, 3 September 1965: *Acta Apostolicae Sedis* 57 (1965), pp. 762-769; Paul VI, Solemn Profession of Faith, *Sollemnis professio fidei*, 30 June 1968, nos. 24-26: *Acta Apostolicae Sedis* 60 (1968), pp. 442-443; Sacred Congregation of Rites, Instruction, *Eucharisticum mysterium*, 25 May 1967, nos. 3f, 9: *Acta Apostolicae Sedis* 59 (1967), pp. 543, 547.

as the Council of Trent proposed that it must be believed,[8] is proclaimed in the celebration of the Mass, not only by the very words of consecration by which Christ is rendered present through transubstantiation, but also with a sense and a demonstration of the greatest reverence and adoration which strives for realization in the Eucharistic liturgy. For the same reason, the Christian people are led to worship this wondrous Sacrament through adoration in a special way on Thursday of the Lord's Supper in Holy Week and on the Solemnity of the Most Holy Body and Blood of Christ.

4.   In truth, the nature of the ministerial priesthood proper to the Bishop and the Priest, who offer the Sacrifice in the person of Christ and who preside over the gathering of the holy people, shines forth in the form of the rite itself, on account of the more prominent place and function given to the Priest. The essential elements of this function are set out and explained clearly and extensively in the Preface for the Chrism Mass on Thursday of Holy Week, the day, namely, when the institution of the priesthood is commemorated. For in the Preface is made clear how the conferral of priestly power is accomplished through the laying on of hands; and, by the listing one by one of its duties, that power is described which is the continuation of the power of Christ, the High Priest of the New Testament.

5.   Moreover, by this nature of the ministerial priesthood, something else is put in its proper light, something certainly to be held in great esteem, namely, the royal priesthood of the faithful, whose spiritual sacrifice is brought to completion through the ministry of the Bishop and the Priests, in union with the Sacrifice of Christ, the sole Mediator.[9] For the celebration of the Eucharist is the action of the whole Church, and in it each one should carry out solely but totally that which pertains to him, in virtue of the place of each within the People

---

[8]   Cf. Ecumenical Council of Trent, Session XIII, 11 October 1551: Denzinger-Schönmetzer, nos. 1635-1661.

[9]   Cf. Second Ecumenical Council of the Vatican, Decree on the Ministry and Life of Priests, *Presbyterorum ordinis*, no. 2.

of God. The result of this is that greater consideration is also given to some aspects of the celebration that have sometimes been accorded less attention in the course of the centuries. For this people is the People of God, purchased by Christ's Blood, gathered together by the Lord, nourished by his word, the people called to present to God the prayers of the entire human family, a people that gives thanks in Christ for the mystery of salvation by offering his Sacrifice, a people, finally, that is brought together in unity by Communion in the Body and Blood of Christ. This people, though holy in its origin, nevertheless grows constantly in holiness by conscious, active, and fruitful participation in the mystery of the Eucharist.[10]

Uninterrupted Tradition

6.   When it set out its instructions for the renewal of the Order of Mass, the Second Vatican Council, using, namely, the same words as did St. Pius V in the Apostolic Constitution *Quo primum*, by which the Missal of Trent was promulgated in 1570, also ordered, among other things, that a number of rites be restored 'to the original norm of the holy Fathers'.[11] From the fact that the same words are used, it can be noted how the two Roman Missals, although four centuries have intervened, embrace one and the same tradition. Furthermore, if the inner elements of this tradition are reflected upon, it is also understood how outstandingly and felicitously the older Roman Missal is brought to fulfilment in the later one.

7.   In truly difficult times, when the Catholic faith in the sacrificial nature of the Mass, the ministerial priesthood, and the real and perpetual presence of Christ under the Eucharistic species were called into question, St. Pius V was first of all concerned with preserving the more recent tradition, then unjustly assailed, introducing only very slight changes into the sacred rite. In fact, the Missal of 1570 differs very little from

---

[10] Cf. Second Ecumenical Council of the Vatican, Constitution on the Sacred Liturgy, *Sacrosanctum Concilium*, no. 11.

[11] *Ibidem*, no. 50.

the very first printed edition of 1474, which in turn faithfully takes up again the Missal used in the time of Pope Innocent III. Moreover, manuscript books in the Vatican Library, even though they provided material for several textual emendations, by no means made it possible to pursue inquiry into 'ancient and approved authors' further back than the liturgical commentaries of the Middle Ages.

8.   Today, however, innumerable writings of scholars have shed light on the 'norm of the holy Fathers' which the revisers of the Missal of St. Pius V assiduously followed. For following the first publication in 1571 of the Sacramentary called the Gregorian, critical editions of other ancient Roman and Ambrosian Sacramentaries were disseminated, often in printed form, as were ancient Hispanic and Gallican liturgical books; these editions brought to light numerous prayers of no slight spiritual value but previously unknown.

In the same way, traditions of the first centuries, before the rites of East and West were formed, are now better known because of the discovery of so many liturgical documents.

Furthermore, continuing progress in the study of the holy Fathers has also shed upon the theology of the mystery of the Eucharist the light brought by the doctrine of such illustrious Fathers of Christian antiquity as St. Irenaeus, St. Ambrose, St. Cyril of Jerusalem, and St. John Chrysostom.

9.   Hence, the 'norm of the holy Fathers' requires not only the preservation of what our immediate forebears have handed on to us, but also an understanding and a more profound pondering of the Church's entire past ages and of all the ways in which her one faith has been expressed in forms of human and social culture so greatly differing among themselves, indeed, as those prevailing in the Semitic, Greek, and Latin regions. Moreover, this broader view allows us to see how the Holy Spirit endows the People of God with a marvellous fidelity in preserving the unalterable deposit of faith, even though there is a very great variety of prayers and rites.

Accommodation to New Conditions

10. Hence, the new Missal, while bearing witness to the Roman Church's rule of prayer (*lex orandi*), also safeguards the deposit of faith handed down by the more recent Councils and marks in its turn a step of great importance in liturgical tradition.

For, when the Fathers of the Second Vatican Council reaffirmed the dogmatic pronouncements of the Council of Trent, they spoke at a far different time in world history, and, for that reason, were able to bring forward proposals and measures regarding pastoral life that could not have even been foreseen four centuries earlier.

11. The Council of Trent had already recognized the great catechetical usefulness contained in the celebration of Mass but was unable to bring out all its consequences in regard to actual practice. In fact, many at that time requested that permission be given to use the vernacular in celebrating the Eucharistic Sacrifice. To such a request, the Council, by reason of the circumstances of that age, judged it a matter of duty to answer by insisting once more on the teaching of the Church as had been handed on, according to which the Eucharistic Sacrifice is in the first place the action of Christ himself, whose inherent efficacy is therefore unaffected by the manner in which the faithful participate in it. The Council for this reason stated in these firm and likewise measured words: 'Although the Mass contains much instruction for the faithful people, it did not seem to the Fathers expedient, however, that it be celebrated indiscriminately in the vernacular'.[12] And the Council declared worthy of censure anyone maintaining that 'the rite of the Roman Church, in which part of the Canon and the words of consecration are pronounced in a low voice, is to be condemned, or that the Mass must be celebrated only in the vernacular'.[13] Nevertheless, at the same time as it prohibited the use of the vernacular in the Mass, it ordered, on the other hand, pastors

---

[12] Ecumenical Council of Trent, Session XXII, *Doctrina de ss. Missae sacrificio*, cap. 8, 17 September 1562: Denzinger-Schönmetzer, no. 1749.

[13] *Ibidem*, cap. 9: Denzinger-Schönmetzer, no. 1759.

of souls to put appropriate catechesis in its place: 'lest Christ's flock go hungry... the Holy Synod commands pastors and each and all of those others having the care of souls that frequently during the celebration of Mass, either personally or through others, they should explain what is read at Mass; and expound, among other things, something of the mystery of this most holy Sacrifice, especially on Sundays and feast days'.[14]

12. Hence, the Second Vatican Council, having come together in order to accommodate the Church to the requirements of her proper apostolic office precisely in these times, considered thoroughly, as had the Council of Trent, the catechetical and pastoral character of the Sacred Liturgy.[15] And since no Catholic would now deny a sacred rite celebrated in Latin to be legitimate and efficacious, the Council was also able to concede that 'not rarely adopting the vernacular language may be of great usefulness for the people' and gave permission for it to be used.[16] The eagerness with which this measure was everywhere received has certainly been so great that it has led, under the guidance of the Bishops and the Apostolic See itself, to permission for all liturgical celebrations in which the people participate to be in the vernacular, so that the people may more fully understand the mystery which is celebrated.

13. In this regard, although the use of the vernacular in the Sacred Liturgy is a means, admittedly of great importance, for expressing more clearly catechesis on the mystery, a catechesis inherent in the celebration itself, the Second Vatican Council ordered additionally that certain prescriptions of the Council of Trent that had not been followed everywhere be brought to fruition, such as the Homily to be given on Sundays and feast

---

[14] *Ibidem*, cap. 8: Denzinger-Schönmetzer, no. 1749.

[15] Cf. Second Ecumenical Council of the Vatican, Constitution on the Sacred Liturgy, *Sacrosanctum Concilium*, no. 33.

[16] *Ibidem*, no. 36.

days[17] and the faculty to interject certain explanations during the sacred rites themselves.[18]

Above all, the Second Vatican Council, which recommended 'that more perfect form of participation in the Mass by which the faithful, after the Priest's Communion, receive the Lord's Body from the same Sacrifice',[19] called for another desire of the Fathers of Trent to be put into effect, namely, that for the sake of a fuller participation in the Holy Eucharist 'at each Mass the faithful present should communicate not only by spiritual desire but also by sacramental reception of the Eucharist'.[20]

14.   Prompted by the same intention and pastoral zeal, the Second Vatican Council was able to give renewed consideration to what was established by Trent on Communion under both kinds. And indeed, since nowadays the doctrinal principles on the complete efficacy of Eucharistic Communion received under the species of bread alone are not in any way called into question, the Council gave permission for the reception on occasion of Communion under both kinds, because this clearer form of the sacramental sign offers a particular opportunity for understanding more deeply the mystery in which the faithful participate.[21]

15.   In this manner the Church, while remaining faithful to her office as teacher of truth, safeguarding 'things old', that is, the deposit of tradition, fulfils at the same time the duty of examining and prudently adopting 'things new' (cf. *Mt* 13:52).

For part of the new Missal orders the prayers of the Church in a way more open to the needs of our times. Of this kind are above all the Ritual Masses and Masses for Various Needs, in

---

[17]   *Ibidem*, no. 52.

[18]   *Ibidem*, no. 35, 3.

[19]   *Ibidem*, no. 55.

[20]   Ecumenical Council of Trent, Session XXII, *Doctrina de ss. Missae sacrificio*, cap. 6: Denzinger-Schönmetzer, no. 1747.

[21]   Cf. Second Ecumenical Council of the Vatican, Constitution on the Sacred Liturgy, *Sacrosanctum Concilium*, no. 55.

which tradition and new elements are appropriately brought together. Thus, while a great number of expressions, drawn from the Church's most ancient tradition and familiar through the many editions of the Roman Missal, have remained unchanged, numerous others have been accommodated to the needs and conditions proper to our own age, and still others, such as the prayers for the Church, for the laity, for the sanctification of human labour, for the community of all nations, and certain needs proper to our era, have been newly composed, drawing on the thoughts and often the very phrasing of the recent documents of the Council.

On account, moreover, of the same attitude toward the new state of the world as it now is, it seemed to cause no harm at all to so revered a treasure if some phrases were changed so that the language would be in accord with that of modern theology and would truly reflect the current state of the Church's discipline. Hence, several expressions regarding the evaluation and use of earthly goods have been changed, as have several which alluded to a certain form of outward penance which was proper to other periods of the Church's past.

In this way, finally, the liturgical norms of the Council of Trent have certainly been completed and perfected in many particulars by those of the Second Vatican Council, which has carried into effect the efforts to bring the faithful closer to the Sacred Liturgy that have been taken up these last four centuries and especially those of recent times, and above all the attention to the Liturgy promoted by St. Pius X and his Successors.

CHAPTER I

THE IMPORTANCE AND DIGNITY OF THE CELEBRATION OF THE EUCHARIST

16.   The celebration of Mass, as the action of Christ and of the People of God arrayed hierarchically, is the centre of the whole of Christian life for the Church both universal and local, as well as for each of the faithful individually.[22] For in it is found the high point both of the action by which God sanctifies the world in Christ and of the worship that the human race offers to the Father, adoring him through Christ, the Son of God, in the Holy Spirit.[23] In it, moreover, during the course of the year, the mysteries of redemption are celebrated so as to be in some way made present.[24] As to the other sacred actions and all the activities of the Christian life, these are bound up with it, flow from it, and are ordered to it.[25]

17.   It is, therefore, of the greatest importance that the celebration of the Mass or the Lord's Supper be so ordered that the sacred ministers and the faithful taking part in it, according to the state proper to each, may draw from it more abundantly[26] those fruits to obtain which Christ the Lord instituted the Eucharistic Sacrifice of his Body and Blood and entrusted it as

---

[22]   Cf. Second Ecumenical Council of the Vatican, Constitution on the Sacred Liturgy, *Sacrosanctum Concilium*, no. 41; Dogmatic Constitution on the Church, *Lumen gentium*, no. 11; Decree on the Ministry and Life of Priests, *Presbyterorum ordinis*, nos. 2, 5, 6; Decree on the Pastoral Office of Bishops, *Christus Dominus*, no. 30; Decree on Ecumenism, *Unitatis redintegratio*, no. 15; Sacred Congregation of Rites, Instruction, *Eucharisticum mysterium*, 25 May 1967, nos. 3e, 6: *Acta Apostolicae Sedis* 59 (1967), pp. 542, 544-545.

[23]   Cf. Second Ecumenical Council of the Vatican, Constitution on the Sacred Liturgy, *Sacrosanctum Concilium*, no. 10.

[24]   Cf. *ibidem*, no. 102.

[25]   Cf. Second Ecumenical Council of the Vatican, Constitution on the Sacred Liturgy, *Sacrosanctum Concilium*, no. 10; cf. Decree on the Ministry and Life of Priests, *Presbyterorum ordinis*, no. 5.

[26]   Cf. Second Ecumenical Council of the Vatican, Constitution on the Sacred Liturgy, *Sacrosanctum Concilium*, nos. 14, 19, 26, 28, 30.

the memorial of his Passion and Resurrection to the Church, his beloved Bride.[27]

18.　This will fittingly come about if, with due regard for the nature and other circumstances of each liturgical assembly, the entire celebration is arranged in such a way that it leads to a conscious, active, and full participation of the faithful, namely in body and in mind, a participation fervent with faith, hope, and charity, of the sort which is desired by the Church and which is required by the very nature of the celebration and to which the Christian people have a right and duty in virtue of their Baptism.[28]

19.　Even though it is on occasion not possible to have the presence and active participation of the faithful, which manifest more clearly the ecclesial nature of the celebration,[29] the celebration of the Eucharist is always endowed with its own efficacy and dignity, since it is the act of Christ and of the Church, in which the Priest fulfils his own principal function and always acts for the sake of the people's salvation.

　　Hence the Priest is recommended to celebrate the Eucharistic Sacrifice, insofar as he can, even daily.[30]

20.　Since, however, the celebration of the Eucharist, like the entire Liturgy, is carried out by means of perceptible signs by which the faith is nourished, strengthened, and expressed,[31] the greatest care is to be taken that those forms and elements proposed by the Church are chosen and arranged, which, given the circumstances of persons and places, more effectively foster active and full participation and more aptly respond to the spiritual needs of the faithful.

---

[27] Cf. *ibidem*, no. 47.

[28] Cf. *ibidem*, no. 14.

[29] Cf. *ibidem*, no. 41.

[30] Cf. Second Ecumenical Council of the Vatican, Decree on the Ministry and Life of Priests, *Presbyterorum ordinis*, no. 13; Code of Canon Law, *Codex Iuris Canonici*, can. 904.

[31] Cf. Second Ecumenical Council of the Vatican, Constitution on the Sacred Liturgy, *Sacrosanctum Concilium*, no. 59.

21.   Hence this Instruction aims both to offer general lines for a suitable ordering of the celebration of the Eucharist and to explain the rules by which individual forms of celebration may be arranged.[32]

22.   The celebration of the Eucharist in a particular Church is of the utmost importance.

For the Diocesan Bishop, the prime steward of the mysteries of God in the particular Church entrusted to his care, is the moderator, promoter, and guardian of the whole of liturgical life.[33] In celebrations that take place with the Bishop presiding, and especially in the celebration of the Eucharist by the Bishop himself with the Presbyterate, the Deacons, and the people taking part, the mystery of the Church is manifest. Hence, solemn celebrations of Mass of this sort must be exemplary for the entire diocese.

The Bishop should therefore be determined that the Priests, the Deacons, and the lay Christian faithful grasp ever more deeply the genuine significance of the rites and liturgical texts, and thereby be led to the active and fruitful celebration of the Eucharist. To that end, he should also be vigilant in ensuring that the dignity of these celebrations be enhanced and, in promoting such dignity, the beauty of the sacred place, of the music, and of art should contribute as greatly as possible.

23.   Moreover, in   order   that   such   a   celebration   may correspond more fully to the prescriptions and spirit of the

---

[32]   Special celebrations of Mass should observe the guidelines established for them: For Masses with particular groups, cf. Sacred Congregation for Divine Worship, Instruction, *Actio pastoralis*, 15 May 1969: *Acta Apostolicae Sedis* 61 (1969), pp. 806-811; for Masses with children, cf. Sacred Congregation for Divine Worship, *Directory for Masses with Children*, 1 November 1973: *Acta Apostolicae Sedis* 66 (1974), pp. 30-46; for the manner of joining the Hours of the Office with the Mass, cf. Sacred Congregation for Divine Worship, *General Instruction of the Liturgy of the Hours*, nos. 93-98; for the manner of joining certain blessings and the crowning of an image of the Blessed Virgin Mary with the Mass, cf. Rituale Romanum, *De Benedictionibus*, editio typica, 1984, Praenotanda, no. 28; *Ordo coronandi imaginem beatae Mariae Virginis*, editio typica, 1981, nos. 10 and 14.

[33]   Cf. Second Ecumenical Council of the Vatican, Decree on the Pastoral Office of Bishops, *Christus Dominus*, no. 15; cf. also Constitution on the Sacred Liturgy, *Sacrosanctum Concilium*, no. 41.

Sacred Liturgy, and also in order that its pastoral effectiveness be enhanced, certain accommodations and adaptations are set out in this General Instruction and in the Order of Mass.

24.   These adaptations consist, for the most part, in the choice of certain rites or texts, that is, of the chants, readings, prayers, explanatory interventions, and gestures capable of responding better to the needs, the preparation, and the culture of the participants and which are entrusted to the Priest Celebrant. However, the Priest will remember that he is the servant of the Sacred Liturgy and that he himself is not permitted, on his own initiative, to add, to remove, or to change anything in the celebration of Mass.[34]

25.   In addition, at the proper place in the Missal are indicated certain adaptations which in accordance with the Constitution on the Sacred Liturgy pertain respectively to the Diocesan Bishop or to the Conference of Bishops[35] (cf. below nos. 387, 388–393).

26.   As for variations and the more profound adaptations which give consideration to the traditions and culture of peoples and regions, to be introduced in accordance with article 40 of the Constitution on the Sacred Liturgy, for reasons of usefulness or necessity, those norms set out in the *Instruction on the Roman Liturgy and Inculturation*[36] and below in nos. 395–399 are to be observed.

---

[34]   Cf. Second Ecumenical Council of the Vatican, Constitution on the Sacred Liturgy, *Sacrosanctum Concilium*, no. 22.

[35]   Cf. Second Ecumenical Council of the Vatican, Constitution on the Sacred Liturgy. *Sacrosanctum Concilium*, nos. 38, 40; Paul VI, Apostolic Constitution, *Missale Romanum*, above.

[36]   Congregation for Divine Worship and the Discipline of the Sacraments, Instruction, *Varietates legitimae*, 25 January 1994: *Acta Apostolicae Sedis* 87 (1995), pp. 288-314.

CHAPTER II

THE STRUCTURE OF THE MASS, ITS ELEMENTS AND ITS PARTS

I. THE GENERAL STRUCTURE OF THE MASS

27.   At Mass or the Lord's Supper the People of God is called together, with a Priest presiding and acting in the person of Christ, to celebrate the memorial of the Lord or Eucharistic Sacrifice.[37] In an outstanding way there applies to such a local gathering of the holy Church the promise of Christ: 'Where two or three are gathered in my name, there am I in their midst' (*Mt* 18:20). For in the celebration of Mass, in which the Sacrifice of the Cross is perpetuated,[38] Christ is really present in the very assembly gathered in his name, in the person of the minister, in his word, and indeed substantially and uninterruptedly under the Eucharistic species.[39]

28.   The Mass consists in some sense of two parts, namely the Liturgy of the Word and the Liturgy of the Eucharist, these being so closely interconnected that they form but one single act of worship.[40] For in the Mass is spread the table both of God's Word and of the Body of Christ, and from it the faithful

---

[37]   Cf. Second Ecumenical Council of the Vatican, Decree on the Ministry and Life of Priests, *Presbyterorum ordinis*, no. 5; Constitution on the Sacred Liturgy, *Sacrosanctum Concilium*, no. 33.

[38]   Cf. Ecumenical Council of Trent, Session XXII, *Doctrina de ss. Missae sacrificio*, cap. 1: Denzinger-Schönmetzer, no. 1740; Paul VI, Solemn Profession of Faith, *Sollemnis professio fidei*, 30 June 1968, no. 24: *Acta Apostolicae Sedis* 60 (1968), p. 442.

[39]   Cf. Second Ecumenical Council of the Vatican, Constitution on the Sacred Liturgy, *Sacrosanctum Concilium*, no. 7; Paul VI, Encyclical Letter, *Mysterium fidei*, 3 September 1965: *Acta Apostolicae Sedis* 57 (1965), p. 764; Sacred Congregation of Rites, Instruction, *Eucharisticum mysterium*, 25 May 1967, no. 9: *Acta Apostolicae Sedis* 59 (1967), p. 547.

[40]   Cf. Second Ecumenical Council of the Vatican, Constitution on the Sacred Liturgy, *Sacrosanctum Concilium*, no. 56; Sacred Congregation of Rites, Instruction, *Eucharisticum mysterium*, 25 May 1967, no. 3: *Acta Apostolicae Sedis* 59 (1967), p. 542.

are to be instructed and refreshed.[41] There are also certain rites that open and conclude the celebration.

II. THE DIFFERENT ELEMENTS OF THE MASS

Reading and Explaining the Word of God

29.   When the Sacred Scriptures are read in the Church, God himself speaks to his people, and Christ, present in his word, proclaims the Gospel.

Therefore, the readings from the Word of God are to be listened to reverently by everyone, for they are an element of the greatest importance in the Liturgy. Although in the readings from Sacred Scripture the Word of God is addressed to all people of whatever era and is understandable to them, a fuller understanding and a greater efficaciousness of the word is nevertheless fostered by a living commentary on the word, that is, by the Homily, as part of the liturgical action.[42]

The Prayers and Other Parts Pertaining to the Priest

30.   Among those things assigned to the Priest, the prime place is occupied by the Eucharistic Prayer, which is the high point of the whole celebration. Next are the orations, that is to say, the Collect, the Prayer over the Offerings, and the Prayer after Communion. These prayers are addressed to God by the Priest who presides over the assembly in the person of Christ, in the name of the entire holy people and of all present.[43] Hence they are rightly called the 'presidential prayers'.

31.   Likewise it is also for the Priest, in the exercise of his office of presiding over the gathered assembly, to offer certain

---

[41] Cf. Second Ecumenical Council of the Vatican, Constitution on the Sacred Liturgy, *Sacrosanctum Concilium*, nos. 48, 51; Dogmatic Constitution on Divine Revelation, *Dei Verbum*, no. 21; Decree on the Ministry and Life of Priests, *Presbyterorum ordinis*, no. 4.

[42] Cf. Second Ecumenical Council of the Vatican, Constitution on the Sacred Liturgy, *Sacrosanctum Concilium*, nos. 7, 33, 52.

[43] Cf. *ibidem*, no. 33.

explanations that are foreseen in the rite itself. Where this is laid down by the rubrics, the celebrant is permitted to adapt them somewhat so that they correspond to the capacity for understanding of those participating. However, the Priest should always take care to keep to the sense of the explanatory text given in the Missal and to express it in just a few words. It is also for the presiding Priest to regulate the Word of God and to impart the final blessing. He is permitted, furthermore, in a very few words, to give the faithful an introduction to the Mass of the day (after the initial Greeting and before the Penitential Act), to the Liturgy of the Word (before the readings), and to the Eucharistic Prayer (before the Preface), though never during the Eucharistic Prayer itself; he may also make concluding comments regarding the entire sacred action before the Dismissal.

32.   The nature of the 'presidential' parts requires that they be spoken in a loud and clear voice and that everyone listen to them attentively.[44] Therefore, while the Priest is pronouncing them, there should be no other prayers or singing, and the organ or other musical instruments should be silent.

33.   For the Priest, as the one who presides, expresses prayers in the name of the Church and of the assembled community; but at times he prays only in his own name, asking that he may exercise his ministry with greater attention and devotion. Prayers of this kind, which occur before the reading of the Gospel, at the Preparation of the Gifts, and also before and after the Communion of the Priest, are said quietly.

Other Formulas Occurring during the Celebration

34.   Since the celebration of Mass by its nature has a 'communitarian' character,[45] both the dialogues between the Priest and the assembled faithful, and the acclamations are of

---

[44] Cf. Sacred Congregation of Rites, Instruction, *Musicam sacram*, 5 March 1967, no. 14: *Acta Apostolicae Sedis* 59 (1967), p. 304.

[45] Cf. Second Ecumenical Council of the Vatican, Constitution on the Sacred Liturgy, *Sacrosanctum Concilium*, nos. 26-27; Sacred Congregation of Rites, Instruction, *Eucharisticum mysterium*, 25 May 1967, no. 3d: *Acta Apostolicae Sedis* 59 (1967), p. 542.

great significance;[46] for they are not simply outward signs of communal celebration but foster and bring about communion between Priest and people.

35.   The acclamations and the responses of the faithful to the Priest's greetings and prayers constitute that level of active participation that is to be made by the assembled faithful in every form of the Mass, so that the action of the whole community may be clearly expressed and fostered.[47]

36.   Other parts, most useful for expressing and fostering the active participation of the faithful, and which are assigned to the whole gathering, include especially the Penitential Act, the Profession of Faith, the Universal Prayer, and the Lord's Prayer.

37.   Finally, among other formulas:

a) Some constitute an independent rite or act, such as the Gloria in excelsis (*Glory to God in the highest*), the Responsorial Psalm, the Alleluia and Verse before the Gospel, the Sanctus (*Holy, Holy, Holy*), the Memorial Acclamation, and the chant after Communion;

b) Others, on the other hand, accompany some other rite, such as the chants at the Entrance, at the Offertory, at the fraction (Agnus Dei, *Lamb of God*) and at Communion.

The Manner of Pronouncing the Different Texts

38.   In texts that are to be pronounced in a loud and clear voice, whether by the Priest or the Deacon, or by a reader, or by everyone, the voice should correspond to the genre of the text itself, that is, depending upon whether it is a reading, a prayer, an explanatory comment, an acclamation, or a sung text; it should also be suited to the form of celebration and to the solemnity of the gathering. Consideration should also be given to the characteristics of different languages and of the culture of different peoples.

---

[46] Cf. Second Ecumenical Council of the Vatican, Constitution on the Sacred Liturgy, *Sacrosanctum Concilium*, no. 30.

[47] Cf. Sacred Congregation of Rites, Instruction, *Musicam sacram*, 5 March 1967, no. 16a: *Acta Apostolicae Sedis* 59 (1967), p. 305.

Therefore, in the rubrics and in the norms that follow, words such as 'say' and 'proclaim' are to be understood either of singing or of reciting, with due regard for the principles stated here above.

The Importance of Singing

39.   The Christian faithful who come together as one in expectation of the Lord's coming are instructed by the Apostle Paul to sing together Psalms, hymns, and spiritual canticles (cf. *Col* 3:16). Singing is the sign of the heart's joy (cf. *Acts* 2:46). Thus St. Augustine says rightly, 'Singing is for one who loves',[48] and there is also an ancient proverb: 'Whoever sings well prays twice over'.

40.   Great importance should therefore be attached to the use of singing in the celebration of the Mass, with due consideration for the culture of peoples and abilities of each liturgical assembly. Although it is not always necessary (e.g., in weekday Masses) to sing all the texts that are in principle meant to be sung, every care should be taken that singing by the ministers and the people not be absent in celebrations that occur on Sundays and on Holydays of Obligation.

However, in the choosing of the parts actually to be sung, preference is to be given to those that are of greater importance and especially to those which are to be sung by the Priest or the Deacon or a reader, with the people replying, or by the Priest and people together.[49]

41.   The main place should be given, all things being equal, to Gregorian chant, as being proper to the Roman Liturgy. Other kinds of sacred music, in particular polyphony, are in no way excluded, provided that they correspond to the spirit of the liturgical action and that they foster the participation of all the faithful.[50]

---

[48]   St. Augustine of Hippo, *Sermo* 336, 1: PL 38, 1472.

[49]   Cf. Sacred Congregation of Rites, Instruction, *Musicam sacram*, 5 March 1967, nos. 7, 16: *Acta Apostolicae Sedis* 59 (1967), pp. 302, 305.

[50]   Cf. Second Ecumenical Council of the Vatican, Constitution on the Sacred Liturgy, *Sacrosanctum Concilium*, no. 116; cf. also no. 30.

Since the faithful from different countries come together ever more frequently, it is desirable that they know how to sing together at least some parts of the Ordinary of the Mass in Latin, especially the Profession of Faith and the Lord's Prayer, according to the simpler settings.[51]

Gestures and Bodily Posture

42.   The gestures and bodily posture of both the Priest, the Deacon, and the ministers, and also of the people, must be conducive to making the entire celebration resplendent with beauty and noble simplicity, to making clear the true and full meaning of its different parts, and to fostering the participation of all.[52] Attention must therefore be paid to what is determined by this General Instruction and by the traditional practice of the Roman Rite and to what serves the common spiritual good of the People of God, rather than private inclination or arbitrary choice.

A common bodily posture, to be observed by all those taking part, is a sign of the unity of the members of the Christian community gathered together for the Sacred Liturgy, for it expresses the intentions and spiritual attitude of the participants and also fosters them.

43.   The faithful should stand from the beginning of the Entrance Chant, or while the Priest approaches the altar, until the end of the Collect; for the Alleluia Chant before the Gospel; while the Gospel itself is proclaimed; during the Profession of Faith and the Universal Prayer; and from the invitation, Orate, fratres (*Pray, brethren*), before the Prayer over the Offerings until the end of Mass, except at the places indicated here below.

---

[51] Cf. Second Ecumenical Council of the Vatican, Constitution on the Sacred Liturgy, *Sacrosanctum Concilium*, no. 54; Sacred Congregation of Rites, Instruction, *Inter Oecumenici*, 26 September 1964, no. 59: *Acta Apostolicae Sedis* 56 (1964), p. 891; Instruction, *Musicam sacram*, 5 March 1967, no. 47: *Acta Apostolicae Sedis* 59 (1967), p. 314.

[52] Cf. Second Ecumenical Council of the Vatican, Constitution on the Sacred Liturgy, *Sacrosanctum Concilium*, nos. 30, 34; cf. also no. 21.

The faithful should sit, on the other hand, during the readings before the Gospel and the Responsorial Psalm and for the Homily and during the Preparation of the Gifts at the Offertory; and, if appropriate, during the period of sacred silence after Communion.

They should kneel, on the other hand, at the Consecration, except when prevented on occasion by ill health, or for reasons of lack of space, of the large number of people present, or for another reasonable cause. However, those who do not kneel ought to make a profound bow when the Priest genuflects after the Consecration.

It is for the Conference of Bishops, in accordance with the norm of law, to adapt the gestures and bodily postures described in the Order of Mass to the culture and reasonable traditions of peoples.[53] However, attention must be paid to ensuring that such adaptations correspond to the meaning and character of each part of the celebration. Where it is the practice for the people to remain kneeling after the Sanctus (*Holy, Holy, Holy*) until the end of the Eucharistic Prayer and before Communion when the Priest says Ecce Agnus Dei (*Behold the Lamb of God*), it is laudable for this practice to be retained.

For the sake of uniformity in gestures and bodily postures during one and the same celebration, the faithful should follow the instructions which the Deacon, a lay minister, or the Priest gives, according to what is laid down in the Missal.

44.   Among gestures are included also actions and processions, by which the Priest, with the Deacon and ministers, goes to the altar; the Deacon carries the Evangeliary or Book of the Gospels to the ambo before the proclamation of the Gospel; the faithful bring up the gifts and come forward to receive Communion. It is appropriate that actions and processions of this sort be carried out with decorum while the chants proper to them are sung, in accordance with the norms laid down for each.

---

[53] Cf. *ibidem,* no. 40; Congregation for Divine Worship and the Discipline of the Sacraments, Instruction, *Varietates legitimae,* 25 January 1994, no. 41: *Acta Apostolicae Sedis* 87 (1995), p. 304.

Silence

45.   Sacred silence also, as part of the celebration, is to be observed at the designated times.[54] Its nature, however, depends on the moment when it occurs in the different parts of the celebration. For in the Penitential Act and again after the invitation to pray, individuals recollect themselves; whereas after a reading or after the Homily, all meditate briefly on what they have heard; then after Communion, they praise God in their hearts and pray to him.

Even before the celebration itself, it is a praiseworthy practice for silence to be observed in the church, in the sacristy, in the vesting room, and in adjacent areas, so that all may dispose themselves to carry out the sacred celebration in a devout and fitting manner.

III. THE INDIVIDUAL PARTS OF THE MASS

A) THE INTRODUCTORY RITES

46.   The rites that precede the Liturgy of the Word, namely, the Entrance, the Greeting, the Penitential Act, the Kyrie, the Gloria in excelsis (*Glory to God in the highest*) and Collect, have the character of a beginning, an introduction, and a preparation.

Their purpose is to ensure that the faithful, who come together as one, establish communion and dispose themselves properly to listen to the Word of God and to celebrate the Eucharist worthily.

In certain celebrations that are combined with Mass according to the norms of the liturgical books, the Introductory Rites are omitted or take place in a particular way.

---

[54] Cf. Second Ecumenical Council of the Vatican, Constitution on the Sacred Liturgy, *Sacrosanctum Concilium*, no. 30; Sacred Congregation of Rites, Instruction, *Musicam sacram*, 5 March 1967, no. 17: *Acta Apostolicae Sedis* 59 (1967), p. 305.

41

The Entrance

47. When the people are gathered, and as the Priest enters with the Deacon and ministers, the Entrance Chant begins. Its purpose is to open the celebration, foster the unity of those who have been gathered, introduce their thoughts to the mystery of the liturgical time or festivity, and accompany the procession of the Priest and ministers.

48. This chant is sung alternately by the choir and the people or similarly by a cantor and the people, or entirely by the people, or by the choir alone. It is possible to use the antiphon with its Psalm from the *Graduale Romanum* or the *Graduale Simplex*, or another chant that is suited to the sacred action, the day, or the time of year,[55] and whose text has been approved by the Conference of Bishops.

If there is no singing at the Entrance, the antiphon given in the Missal is recited either by the faithful, or by some of them, or by a reader; otherwise, it is recited by the Priest himself, who may even adapt it as an introductory explanation (*cf. no. 31*).

In England and Wales: This chant is sung alternately by the choir and the people or similarly by a cantor and the people, or entirely by the people, or by the choir alone. In the dioceses of England and Wales the Entrance Chant may be chosen from among the following: the antiphon with its Psalm from the *Graduale Romanum* or the *Graduale Simplex*, or another chant that is suited to the sacred action, the day, or the time of year, and whose text has been approved by the Conference of Bishops of England and Wales.

If there is no singing at the Entrance, the antiphon given in the Missal is recited either by the faithful, or by some of them, or by a reader; otherwise, it is recited by the Priest himself, who may even adapt it as an introductory explanation (*cf. no. 31*).

---

[55] Cf. John Paul II, Apostolic Letter, *Dies Domini*, 31 May 1998, no. 50: *Acta Apostolicae Sedis* 90 (1998), p. 745.

In Scotland: This chant is sung alternately by the choir and the people or similarly by a cantor and the people, or entirely by the people, or by the choir alone. In the dioceses of Scotland the Entrance Chant may be chosen from among the following: the antiphon with its Psalm from the *Graduale Romanum* or the *Graduale Simplex*, or another chant that is suited to the sacred action, the day, or the time of year, and whose text has been approved by the Conference of Bishops of Scotland.

If there is no singing at the Entrance, the antiphon given in the Missal is recited either by the faithful, or by some of them, or by a reader; otherwise, it is recited by the Priest himself, who may even adapt it as an introductory explanation (*cf. no. 31*).

Reverence to the Altar and Greeting of the Assembled People

49.   When they have arrived at the sanctuary, the Priest, the Deacon, and the ministers reverence the altar with a profound bow. Moreover, as an expression of veneration, the Priest and Deacon then kiss the altar itself; the Priest, if appropriate, also incenses the cross and the altar.

50.   When the Entrance Chant is concluded, the Priest stands at the chair and, together with the whole gathering, signs himself with the Sign of the Cross. Then by means of the Greeting he signifies the presence of the Lord to the assembled community. By this greeting and the people's response, the mystery of the Church gathered together is made manifest.

After the greeting of the people, the Priest, or the Deacon, or a lay minister may very briefly introduce the faithful to the Mass of the day.

The Penitential Act

51.   After this, the Priest calls upon the whole community to take part in the Penitential Act, which, after a brief pause for silence, it does by means of a formula of general confession. The rite concludes with the Priest's absolution, which, however, lacks the efficacy of the Sacrament of Penance.

From time to time on Sundays, especially in Easter Time, instead of the customary Penitential Act, the blessing and sprinkling of water may take place as a reminder of Baptism.[56]

The Kyrie Eleison

52.   After the Penitential Act, the Kyrie, eleison (*Lord, have mercy*), is always begun, unless it has already been part of the Penitential Act. Since it is a chant by which the faithful acclaim the Lord and implore his mercy, it is usually executed by everyone, that is to say, with the people and the choir or cantor taking part in it.

Each acclamation is usually pronounced twice, though it is not to be excluded that it be repeated several times, by reason of the character of the various languages, as well as of the artistry of the music or of other circumstances. When the Kyrie is sung as a part of the Penitential Act, a 'trope' precedes each acclamation.

The Gloria in Excelsis

53.   The Gloria in excelsis (*Glory to God in the highest*) is a most ancient and venerable hymn by which the Church, gathered in the Holy Spirit, glorifies and entreats God the Father and the Lamb. The text of this hymn may not be replaced by any other. It is intoned by the Priest or, if appropriate, by a cantor or by the choir; but it is sung either by everyone together, or by the people alternately with the choir, or by the choir alone. If not sung, it is to be recited either by everybody together or by two choirs responding one to the other.

It is sung or said on Sundays outside Advent and Lent, and also on Solemnities and Feasts, and at particular celebrations of a more solemn character.

The Collect

54.   Next the Priest calls upon the people to pray and everybody, together with the Priest, observes a brief silence so that they may become aware of being in God's presence and

---

[56] Cf. below, pp. 1507-1510.

may call to mind their intentions. Then the Priest pronounces the prayer usually called the 'Collect' and through which the character of the celebration finds expression. By an ancient tradition of the Church, the 'Collect' prayer is usually addressed to God the Father, through Christ, in the Holy Spirit,[57] and is concluded with a Trinitarian ending, or longer ending, in the following manner:

– If the prayer is directed to the Father: Through our Lord Jesus Christ, your Son, who lives and reigns with you in the unity of the Holy Spirit, one God, for ever and ever;

– If it is directed to the Father, but the Son is mentioned at the end: Who lives and reigns with you in the unity of the Holy Spirit, one God, for ever and ever;

– If it is directed to the Son: Who live and reign with God the Father in the unity of the Holy Spirit, one God, for ever and ever.

The people, joining in this petition, make the prayer their own by means of the acclamation Amen.

At Mass only a single Collect is ever said.

B) The Liturgy of the Word

55.   The main part of the Liturgy of the Word is made up of the readings from Sacred Scripture together with the chants occurring between them. As for the Homily, the Profession of Faith and the Universal Prayer, they develop and conclude it. For in the readings, as explained by the Homily, God speaks to his people,[58] opening up to them the mystery of redemption and salvation, and offering spiritual nourishment; and Christ himself is present through his word in the midst of the faithful.[59] By silence and by singing, the people make this divine word their

---

[57] Cf. Tertullian, *Adversus Marcionem*, IV, 9: *Corpus Christianorum, Series Latina* 1, p. 560; Origen, *Disputatio cum Heracleida*, no. 4, 24: *Sources chretiennes* 67, p. 62; *Statuta Concilii Hipponensis Breviata*, no. 21: *Corpus Christianorum, Series Latina* 149, p. 39.

[58] Cf. Second Ecumenical Council of the Vatican, Constitution on the Sacred Liturgy, *Sacrosanctum Concilium*, no. 33.

[59] Cf. *ibidem*, no. 7.

own, and affirm their adherence to it by means of the Profession of Faith; finally, having been nourished by the divine word, the people pour out their petitions by means of the Universal Prayer for the needs of the whole Church and for the salvation of the whole world.

Silence

56.   The Liturgy of the Word is to be celebrated in such a way as to favour meditation, and so any kind of haste such as hinders recollection is clearly to be avoided. In the course of it, brief periods of silence are also appropriate, accommodated to the assembled congregation; by means of these, under the action of the Holy Spirit, the Word of God may be grasped by the heart and a response through prayer may be prepared. It may be appropriate to observe such periods of silence, for example, before the Liturgy of the Word itself begins, after the First and Second Reading, and lastly at the conclusion of the Homily.[60]

The Biblical Readings

57.   In the readings, the table of God's Word is spread before the faithful, and the treasures of the Bible are opened to them.[61] Hence, it is preferable that the arrangement of the biblical readings be maintained, for by them the unity of both Testaments and of salvation history is brought out. Nor is it lawful to replace the readings and Responsorial Psalm, which contain the Word of God, with other, non-biblical texts.[62]

58.   In the celebration of the Mass with the people, the readings are always read from the ambo.

59.   The function of proclaiming the readings is by tradition not presidential but ministerial. Therefore the readings are to be

---

[60] Cf. Missale Romanum, *Ordo lectionum Missae*, editio typica altera, 1981, Praenotanda, no. 28.

[61] Cf. Second Ecumenical Council of the Vatican, Constitution on the Sacred Liturgy, *Sacrosanctum Concilium*, no. 51.

[62] Cf. John Paul II, Apostolic Letter, *Vicesimus quintus annus*, 4 December 1988, no. 13: *Acta Apostolicae Sedis* 81 (1989), p. 910.

read by a reader, but the Gospel by the Deacon or, in his absence, by another Priest. If, however, a Deacon or another Priest is not present, the Priest Celebrant himself should read the Gospel, and moreover, if no other suitable reader is present, the Priest Celebrant should also proclaim the other readings as well.

After each reading, whoever reads it pronounces the acclamation, and by means of the reply the assembled people give honour to the Word of God that they have received in faith and with gratitude.

60.   The reading of the Gospel constitutes the high point of the Liturgy of the Word. The Liturgy itself teaches the great reverence that is to be shown to this reading by setting it off from the other readings with special marks of honour, by the fact of which minister is appointed to proclaim it and by the blessing or prayer with which he prepares himself; and also by the fact that through their acclamations the faithful acknowledge and confess that Christ is present and is speaking to them and stand as they listen to the reading; and by the mere fact of the marks of reverence that are given to the Book of the Gospels.

The Responsorial Psalm

61.   After the First Reading follows the Responsorial Psalm, which is an integral part of the Liturgy of the Word and which has great liturgical and pastoral importance, since it fosters meditation on the Word of God.

The Responsorial Psalm should correspond to each reading and should usually be taken from the Lectionary.

It is preferable for the Responsorial Psalm to be sung, at least as far as the people's response is concerned. Hence the psalmist, or cantor of the Psalm, sings the Psalm verses at the ambo or another suitable place, while the whole congregation sits and listens, normally taking part by means of the response, except when the Psalm is sung straight through, that is, without a response. However, in order that the people may be able to sing the Psalm response more easily, texts of some responses and Psalms have been chosen for the different times of the year or for the different categories of Saints. These may be used instead of the text corresponding to the reading whenever the Psalm is sung. If the Psalm cannot be sung, then it should be recited in a way that is particularly suited to fostering meditation on the Word of God.

Instead of the Psalm assigned in the Lectionary, there may be sung either the Responsorial Gradual from the *Graduale Romanum*, or the Responsorial Psalm or the *Alleluia* Psalm from the *Graduale Simplex*, as described in these books.

The Acclamation before the Gospel

62. After the reading that immediately precedes the Gospel, the Alleluia or another chant laid down by the rubrics is sung, as the liturgical time requires. An acclamation of this kind constitutes a rite or act in itself, by which the gathering of the faithful welcomes and greets the Lord who is about to speak to them in the Gospel and profess their faith by means of the chant. It is sung by everybody, standing, and is led by the choir or a cantor, being repeated as the case requires. The verse, on the other hand, is sung either by the choir or by a cantor.

a) The Alleluia is sung in every time of year other than Lent. The verses are taken from the Lectionary or the *Graduale*.

b) During Lent, instead of the Alleluia, the Verse before the Gospel as given in the Lectionary is sung. It is also possible to sing another Psalm or Tract, as found in the *Graduale*.

63. When there is only one reading before the Gospel:

a) during a time of year when the Alleluia is prescribed, either an Alleluia Psalm or the Responsorial Psalm followed by the Alleluia with its verse may be used;

b) during a time of year when the Alleluia is not foreseen, either the Psalm and the Verse before the Gospel or the Psalm alone may be used;

c) the Alleluia or the Verse before the Gospel, if not sung, may be omitted.

64. The Sequence which, except on Easter Sunday and on Pentecost Day, is optional, is sung before the Alleluia.

The Homily

65.   The Homily is part of the Liturgy and is highly recommended,[63] for it is necessary for the nurturing of the Christian life. It should be an explanation of some aspect of the readings from Sacred Scripture or of another text from the Ordinary or the Proper of the Mass of the day and should take into account both the mystery being celebrated and the particular needs of the listeners.[64]

66.   The Homily should ordinarily be given by the Priest Celebrant himself or be entrusted by him to a concelebrating Priest, or from time to time and, if appropriate, to the Deacon, but never to a lay person.[65] In particular cases and for a just cause, the Homily may even be given by a Bishop or a Priest who is present at the celebration but cannot concelebrate.

On Sundays and Holydays of Obligation there is to be a Homily at every Mass that is celebrated with the people attending and it may not be omitted without a grave reason. On other days it is recommended, especially on the weekdays of Advent, Lent and Easter Time, as well as on other festive days and occasions when the people come to church in greater numbers.[66]

It is appropriate for a brief period of silence to be observed after the Homily.

The Profession of Faith

67.   The purpose of the Symbol or Profession of Faith or Creed, is that the whole gathered people may respond to the Word of

---

[63]   Cf. Second Ecumenical Council of the Vatican, Constitution on the Sacred Liturgy, *Sacrosanctum Concilium*, no. 52; Code of Canon Law, *Codex Iuris Canonici*, can. 767 § 1.

[64]   Cf. Sacred Congregation of Rites, Instruction, *Inter Oecumenici*, 26 September 1964, no. 54: *Acta Apostolicae Sedis* 56 (1964), p. 890

[65]   Cf. Code of Canon Law, *Codex Iuris Canonici*, can. 767 § 1; Pontifical Commission for the Authentic Interpretation of the Code of Canon Law, response to *dubium* regarding can. 767 § 1: *Acta Apostolicae Sedis* 79 (1987), p. 1249; Interdicasterial Instruction on certain questions regarding the collaboration of the non-ordained faithful in the sacred ministry of Priests, *Ecclesiae de mysterio*, 15 August 1997, art. 3: *Acta Apostolicae Sedis* 89 (1997), p. 864.

[66]   Cf. Sacred Congregation of Rites, Instruction, *Inter Oecumenici*, 26 September 1964, no. 53: *Acta Apostolicae Sedis* 56 (1964), p. 890.

God proclaimed in the readings taken from Sacred Scripture and explained in the Homily and that they may also honour and confess the great mysteries of the faith by pronouncing the rule of faith in a formula approved for liturgical use and before the celebration of these mysteries in the Eucharist begins.

68.   The Creed is to be sung or said by the Priest together with the people on Sundays and Solemnities. It may be said also at particular celebrations of a more solemn character.

If it is sung, it is intoned by the Priest or, if appropriate, by a cantor or by the choir. It is then sung either by everybody together or by the people alternating with the choir.

If it is not sung, it is to be recited by everybody together or by two choirs responding one to the other.

The Universal Prayer

69.   In the Universal Prayer or Prayer of the Faithful, the people respond in some sense to the Word of God which they have received in faith and, exercising the office of their baptismal priesthood, offer prayers to God for the salvation of all. It is desirable that there usually be such a form of prayer in Masses celebrated with the people, so that petitions may be offered for holy Church, for those who govern with authority over us, for those weighed down by various needs, for all humanity, and for the salvation of the whole world.[67]

70.   The series of intentions is usually to be:

a) for the needs of the Church;

b) for public authorities and the salvation of the whole world;

c) for those burdened by any kind of difficulty;

d) for the local community.

Nevertheless, in any particular celebration, such as a Confirmation, a Marriage, or at a Funeral, the series of intentions may be concerned more closely with the particular occasion.

---

[67] Cf. Second Ecumenical Council of the Vatican, Constitution on the Sacred Liturgy, *Sacrosanctum Concilium*, no. 53.

71.   It is for the Priest Celebrant to regulate this prayer from the chair. He himself begins it with a brief introduction, by which he calls upon the faithful to pray, and likewise he concludes it with an oration. The intentions announced should be sober, be composed with a wise liberty and in few words, and they should be expressive of the prayer of the entire community.

They are announced from the ambo or from another suitable place, by the Deacon or by a cantor, a reader, or one of the lay faithful.[68]

The people, for their part, stand and give expression to their prayer either by an invocation said in common after each intention or by praying in silence.

C) THE LITURGY OF THE EUCHARIST

72.   At the Last Supper Christ instituted the Paschal Sacrifice and banquet, by which the Sacrifice of the Cross is continuously made present in the Church whenever the Priest, representing Christ the Lord, carries out what the Lord himself did and handed over to his disciples to be done in his memory.[69]

For Christ took the bread and the chalice, gave thanks, broke the bread and gave it to his disciples, saying: Take, eat and drink: this is my Body; this is the chalice of my Blood. Do this in memory of me. Hence, the Church has arranged the entire celebration of the Liturgy of the Eucharist in parts corresponding to precisely these words and actions of Christ, namely:

a) At the Preparation of the Gifts, bread and wine with water are brought to the altar, the same elements, that is to say, which Christ took into his hands.

b) In the Eucharistic Prayer, thanks is given to God for the whole work of salvation, and the offerings become the Body and Blood of Christ.

---

[68] Cf. Sacred Congregation of Rites, Instruction, *Inter Oecumenici*, 26 September 1964, no. 56: *Acta Apostolicae Sedis* 56 (1964), p. 890.

[69] Cf. Second Ecumenical Council of the Vatican, Constitution on the Sacred Liturgy, *Sacrosanctum Concilium*, no. 47; Sacred Congregation of Rites, Instruction, *Eucharisticum mysterium*, 25 May 1967, no. 3a, b: *Acta Apostolicae Sedis* 59 (1967), pp. 540-541.

c) Through the fraction and through Communion, the faithful, though many, receive from the one bread the Lord's Body and from the one chalice the Lord's Blood in the same way that the Apostles received them from the hands of Christ himself.

The Preparation of the Gifts

73.   At the beginning of the Liturgy of the Eucharist the gifts which will become Christ's Body and Blood are brought to the altar.

First of all, the altar or Lord's table, which is the centre of the whole Liturgy of the Eucharist,[70] is made ready when on it are placed the corporal, purificator, Missal and chalice (unless this last is prepared at the credence table).

The offerings are then brought forward. It is a praiseworthy practice for the bread and wine to be presented by the faithful. They are then accepted at an appropriate place by the Priest or the Deacon to be carried to the altar. Even though the faithful no longer bring from their own possessions the bread and wine intended for the liturgy as was once the case, nevertheless the rite of carrying up the offerings still keeps its spiritual efficacy and significance.

Even money or other gifts for the poor or for the Church, brought by the faithful or collected in the church, are acceptable; given their purpose they are to be put in a suitable place away from the Eucharistic table.

74.   The procession bringing the gifts is accompanied by the Offertory Chant (*cf. no. 37 b*), which continues at least until the gifts have been placed on the altar. The norms on the manner of singing are the same as for the Entrance Chant (*cf. no. 48*). Singing may always accompany the rite at the Offertory, even when there is no procession with the gifts.

---

[70] Cf. Sacred Congregation of Rites, Instruction, *Inter Oecumenici*, 26 September 1964, no. 91: *Acta Apostolicae Sedis* 56 (1964), p. 898; Instruction, *Eucharisticum mysterium*, 25 May 1967, no. 24: *Acta Apostolicae Sedis* 59 (1967), p. 554.

75.   The bread and wine are placed on the altar by the Priest to the accompaniment of the prescribed formulas; the Priest may incense the gifts placed on the altar and then incense the cross and the altar itself, so as to signify the Church's offering and prayer rising like incense in the sight of God. Next, the Priest, because of his sacred ministry, and the people, by reason of their baptismal dignity, may be incensed by the Deacon or by another minister.

76.   Then the Priest washes his hands at the side of the altar, a rite in which the desire for interior purification finds expression.

The Prayer over the Offerings

77.   Once the offerings have been placed on the altar and the accompanying rites completed, by means of the invitation to pray with the Priest and by means of the Prayer over the Offerings, the Preparation of the Gifts is concluded and preparation made for the Eucharistic Prayer.

At Mass, a single Prayer over the Offerings is said, and it ends with the shorter conclusion, that is: Through Christ our Lord. If, however, the Son is mentioned at the end of this prayer, the conclusion is: Who lives and reigns for ever and ever.

The people, joining in this petition, make the prayer their own by means of the acclamation Amen.

The Eucharistic Prayer

78.   Now the centre and high point of the entire celebration begins, namely, the Eucharistic Prayer itself, that is, the prayer of thanksgiving and sanctification. The Priest calls upon the people to lift up their hearts towards the Lord in prayer and thanksgiving; he associates the people with himself in the Prayer that he addresses in the name of the entire community to God the Father through Jesus Christ in the Holy Spirit. Furthermore, the meaning of this Prayer is that the whole congregation of the faithful joins with Christ in confessing the great deeds of God and in the offering of Sacrifice. The Eucharistic Prayer requires that everybody listens to it with reverence and in silence.

79.   The main elements of which the Eucharistic Prayer consists may be distinguished from one another in this way:

a) The *thanksgiving* (expressed especially in the Preface), in which the Priest, in the name of the whole of the holy people, glorifies God the Father and gives thanks to him for the whole work of salvation or for some particular aspect of it, according to the varying day, festivity, or time of year.

b) The *acclamation,* by which the whole congregation, joining with the heavenly powers, sings the Sanctus *(Holy, Holy, Holy)*. This acclamation, which constitutes part of the Eucharistic Prayer itself, is pronounced by all the people with the Priest.

c) The *epiclesis*, in which, by means of particular invocations, the Church implores the power of the Holy Spirit that the gifts offered by human hands be consecrated, that is, become Christ's Body and Blood, and that the unblemished sacrificial Victim to be consumed in Communion may be for the salvation of those who will partake of it.

d) The *Institution narrative and Consecration*, by which, by means of the words and actions of Christ, that Sacrifice is effected which Christ himself instituted during the Last Supper, when he offered his Body and Blood under the species of bread and wine, gave them to the Apostles to eat and drink, and leaving with the latter the command to perpetuate this same mystery.

e) The *anamnesis*, by which the Church, fulfilling the command that she received from Christ the Lord through the Apostles, celebrates the memorial of Christ, recalling especially his blessed Passion, glorious Resurrection and Ascension into heaven.

f) The *oblation*, by which, in this very memorial, the Church, in particular that gathered here and now, offers the unblemished sacrificial Victim in the Holy Spirit to the Father. The Church's intention, indeed, is that the faithful not only offer this unblemished sacrificial Victim but also learn to offer their very selves,[71] and so day by day to be brought, through the mediation of Christ, into unity with God and with each other, so that God may at last be all in all.[72]

g) The *intercessions*, by which expression is given to the fact that the Eucharist is celebrated in communion with the whole Church, of both heaven and of earth, and that the oblation is made for her and for all her members, living and dead, who are called to participate in the redemption and salvation purchased by the Body and Blood of Christ.

h) The *concluding doxology*, by which the glorification of God is expressed and which is affirmed and concluded by the people's acclamation Amen.

The Communion Rite

80.   Since the celebration of the Eucharist is the Paschal Banquet, it is desirable that in accordance with the Lord's command his Body and Blood should be received as spiritual food by those of the faithful who are properly disposed. This is the sense of the fraction and the other preparatory rites by which the faithful are led more immediately to Communion.

The Lord's Prayer

81.   In the Lord's Prayer a petition is made for daily bread, which for Christians means principally the Eucharistic Bread, and entreating also purification from sin, so that what is holy may in truth be given to the holy. The Priest pronounces the invitation to the prayer, and all the faithful say the prayer with him; then the Priest alone adds the embolism, which the

---

[71] Cf. Second Ecumenical Council of the Vatican, Constitution on the Sacred Liturgy, *Sacrosanctum Concilium*, no. 48; Sacred Congregation of Rites, Instruction, *Eucharisticum mysterium*, 25 May 1967, no. 12: *Acta Apostolicae Sedis* 59 (1967), pp. 548-549.

[72] Cf. Second Ecumenical Council of the Vatican, Constitution on the Sacred Liturgy, *Sacrosanctum Concilium*, no. 48; Decree on the Ministry and Life of Priests, *Presbyterorum ordinis*, no. 5; Sacred Congregation of Rites, Instruction, *Eucharisticum mysterium*, 25 May 1967, no. 12: *Acta Apostolicae Sedis* 59 (1967), pp. 548-549.

people conclude by means of the doxology. The embolism, developing the last petition of the Lord's Prayer itself, asks for deliverance from the power of evil for the whole community of the faithful.

The invitation, the Prayer itself, the embolism, and the doxology by which the people conclude these things are sung or are said aloud.

The Rite of Peace

82.   There follows the Rite of Peace, by which the Church entreats peace and unity for herself and for the whole human family, and the faithful express to each other their ecclesial communion and mutual charity before communicating in the Sacrament.

As for the actual sign of peace to be given, the manner is to be established by the Conferences of Bishops in accordance with the culture and customs of the peoples. However, it is appropriate that each person, in a sober manner, offer the sign of peace only to those who are nearest.

The Fraction of the Bread

83.   The Priest breaks the Eucharistic Bread, with the assistance, if the case requires, of the Deacon or a concelebrant. The gesture of breaking bread done by Christ at the Last Supper, which in apostolic times gave the entire Eucharistic Action its name, signifies that the many faithful are made one body (1 Cor 10:17) by receiving Communion from the one Bread of Life, which is Christ, who for the salvation of the world died and rose again. The fraction or breaking of bread is begun after the sign of peace and is carried out with proper reverence, and should not be unnecessarily prolonged or accorded exaggerated importance. This rite is reserved to the Priest and the Deacon.

The Priest breaks the Bread and puts a piece of the host into the chalice to signify the unity of the Body and Blood of the Lord in the work of salvation, namely, of the Body of Jesus Christ, living and glorious. The supplication Agnus Dei (*Lamb of God*) is usually sung by the choir or cantor with the congregation replying; or at least recited aloud. This invocation accompanies the fraction of the bread and, for this reason, may be repeated as many times as necessary until the rite has been completed. The final time it concludes with the words grant us peace.

Communion

84.   The Priest prepares himself by a prayer, said quietly, so that he may fruitfully receive the Body and Blood of Christ. The faithful do the same, praying silently.

Then the Priest shows the faithful the Eucharistic Bread, holding it over the paten or over the chalice, and invites them to the banquet of Christ; and along with the faithful, he then makes an act of humility, using the prescribed words from the Gospels.

85.   It is most desirable that the faithful, just as the Priest himself is bound to do, receive the Lord's Body from hosts consecrated at the same Mass and that, in the cases where this is foreseen, they partake of the chalice (*cf. no. 283*), so that even by means of the signs Communion may stand out more clearly as a participation in the sacrifice actually being celebrated.[73]

86.   While the Priest is receiving the Sacrament, the Communion Chant is begun, its purpose being to express the spiritual union of the communicants by means of the unity of their voices, to show gladness of heart, and to bring out more clearly the 'communitarian' character of the procession to receive the Eucharist. The singing is prolonged for as long as the Sacrament is being administered to the faithful.[74] However, if there is to be a hymn after Communion, the Communion Chant should be ended in a timely manner.

Care should be taken that singers, too, can receive Communion with ease.

---

[73] Cf. Sacred Congregation of Rites, Instruction *Eucharisticum mysterium*, 25 May 1967, nos. 31, 32: *Acta Apostolicae Sedis* 59 (1969), pp. 558-559; Sacred Congregation for the Discipline of the Sacraments, Instruction, *Immensae caritatis*, 29 January 1973, no. 2: *Acta Apostolicae Sedis* 65 (1973), pp. 267-268.

[74] Cf. Sacred Congregation for the Sacraments and Divine Worship, Instruction, *Inestimabile donum*, 3 April 1980, no. 17: *Acta Apostolicae Sedis* 72 (1980), p. 338.

87. For singing at Communion, it is possible to use the antiphon from the *Graduale Romanum*, with or without the Psalm, or the antiphon with Psalm from the *Graduale Simplex*, or some other suitable liturgical chant approved by the Conference of Bishops.

This is sung either by the choir alone or by the choir or a cantor with the people.

However, if there is no singing, the antiphon given in the Missal may be recited either by the faithful, or by some of them, or by a reader; otherwise, it is recited by the Priest himself after he has received Communion and before he distributes Communion to the faithful.

In England and Wales: In the dioceses of England and Wales singing at Communion may be chosen from among the following: the antiphon from the *Graduale Romanum*, with or without the Psalm, or the antiphon with Psalm from the *Graduale Simplex*, or some other suitable liturgical chant approved by the Conference of Bishops of England and Wales. This is sung either by the choir alone or by the choir or a cantor with the people.

However, if there is no singing, the antiphon given in the Missal may be recited either by the faithful, or by some of them, or by a reader; otherwise, it is recited by the Priest himself after he has received Communion and before he distributes Communion to the faithful.

In Scotland: In the dioceses of Scotland singing at Communion may be chosen from among the following: the antiphon from the *Graduale Romanum*, with or without the Psalm, or the antiphon with Psalm from the *Graduale Simplex*, or some other suitable liturgical chant approved by the Conference of Bishops of Scotland. This is sung either by the choir alone or by the choir or a cantor with the people.

However, if there is no singing, the antiphon given in the Missal may be recited either by the faithful, or by some of them, or by a reader; otherwise, it is recited by the Priest himself after he has received Communion and before he distributes Communion to the faithful.

88. When the distribution of Communion is over, if appropriate, the Priest and faithful pray quietly for some time. If desired, a Psalm or other canticle of praise or a hymn may also be sung by the whole congregation.

89. To bring to completion the prayer of the People of God, and also to conclude the whole Communion Rite, the Priest pronounces the Prayer after Communion, in which he prays for the fruits of the mystery just celebrated.

At Mass a single Prayer after Communion is said, and it ends with the shorter conclusion; that is:

– if the prayer is directed to the Father: Through Christ our Lord;

– if it is directed to the Father, but the Son is mentioned at the end: Who lives and reigns for ever and ever;

– if it is directed to the Son: Who live and reign for ever and ever.

The people make the prayer their own by means of the acclamation Amen.

D) THE CONCLUDING RITES

90. To the Concluding Rites belong the following:

a) brief announcements, should they be necessary;

b) the Priest's Greeting and Blessing, which on certain days and occasions is expanded and expressed by the Prayer over the People or another more solemn formula;

c) the Dismissal of the people by the Deacon or the Priest, so that each may go back to doing good works, praising and blessing God;

d) the kissing of the altar by the Priest and the Deacon, followed by a profound bow to the altar by the Priest, the Deacon, and the other ministers.

CHAPTER III

DUTIES AND MINISTRIES IN THE MASS

91.   The celebration of the Eucharist is the action of Christ and of the Church, namely, of the holy people united and ordered under the Bishop. It therefore pertains to the whole Body of the Church, manifests it, and has its effect upon it. Indeed, it also affects the individual members of the Church in a different way, according to their different orders, functions, and actual participation.[75] In this way, the Christian people, 'a chosen race, a royal priesthood, a holy nation, a people for his own possession', expresses its cohesion and its hierarchical ordering.[76] All, therefore, whether ordained ministers or lay Christian faithful, in fulfilling their function or their duty, should carry out solely but totally that which pertains to them.[77]

I. THE DUTIES OF THOSE IN HOLY ORDERS

92.   Every legitimate celebration of the Eucharist is directed by the Bishop, either in person or through Priests who are his helpers.[78]

When the Bishop is present at a Mass where the people are gathered, it is most fitting that he himself celebrate the Eucharist and associate Priests with himself in the sacred action as concelebrants. This is done not for the sake of adding outward solemnity to the rite, but to signify more vividly the mystery of the Church, 'the sacrament of unity'.[79]

---

[75] Cf. Second Ecumenical Council of the Vatican, Constitution on the Sacred Liturgy, *Sacrosanctum Concilium*, no. 26.

[76] Cf. *ibidem*, no. 14.

[77] Cf. *ibidem*, no. 28.

[78] Cf. Second Ecumenical Council of the Vatican, Dogmatic Constitution on the Church, *Lumen gentium*, nos. 26, 28; Constitution on the Sacred Liturgy, *Sacrosanctum Concilium*, no. 42.

[79] Cf. Second Ecumenical Council of the Vatican, Constitution on the Sacred Liturgy, *Sacrosanctum Concilium*, no. 26.

If, on the other hand, the Bishop does not celebrate the Eucharist but has assigned it to someone else to do this, then it is appropriate that he should preside over the Liturgy of the Word, wearing the pectoral cross, stole, and cope over an alb, and that he should give the blessing at the end of Mass.[80]

93. A Priest, also, who possesses within the Church the sacred power of Orders to offer sacrifice in the person of Christ,[81] presides by this fact over the faithful people gathered here and now, presides over their prayer, proclaims to them the message of salvation, associates the people with himself in the offering of sacrifice through Christ in the Holy Spirit to God the Father, and gives his brothers and sisters the Bread of eternal life and partakes of it with them. Therefore, when he celebrates the Eucharist, he must serve God and the people with dignity and humility, and by his bearing and by the way he pronounces the divine words he must convey to the faithful the living presence of Christ.

94. After the Priest, the Deacon, in virtue of the sacred Ordination he has received, holds first place among those who minister in the celebration of the Eucharist. For the sacred Order of the Diaconate has been held in high honour in the Church even from the early time of the Apostles.[82] At Mass the Deacon has his own part in proclaiming the Gospel, from time to time in preaching God's Word, in announcing the intentions of the Universal Prayer, in ministering to the Priest, in preparing the altar and in serving the celebration of the Sacrifice, in distributing the Eucharist to the faithful, especially under the species of wine, and from time to time in giving instructions regarding the people's gestures and posture.

---

[80] Cf. *Caeremoniale Episcoporum, editio typica*, 1984, nos. 175-186.

[81] Cf. Second Ecumenical Council of the Vatican, Dogmatic Constitution on the Church, *Lumen gentium*, no. 28; Decree on the Ministry and Life of Priests, *Presbyterorum ordinis*, no. 2.

[82] Cf. Paul VI, Apostolic Letter, *Sacrum Diaconatus Ordinem*, 18 June 1967: *Acta Apostolicae Sedis* 59 (1967), pp. 697-704; Pontificale Romanum, *De Ordinatione Episcopi, presbyterorum et diaconorum*, editio typica altera, 1989, no. 173.

II. THE FUNCTIONS OF THE PEOPLE OF GOD

95.   In the celebration of Mass the faithful form a holy people, a people of God's own possession and a royal priesthood, so that they may give thanks to God and offer the unblemished sacrificial Victim not only by means of the hands of the Priest but also together with him and so that they may learn to offer their very selves.[83] They should, moreover, take care to show this by their deep religious sense and their charity toward brothers and sisters who participate with them in the same celebration.

They are consequently to avoid any appearance of singularity or division, keeping in mind that they have only one Father in heaven and that hence are all brothers or sisters one to the other.

96.   Moreover, they are to form one body, whether in hearing the Word of God, or in taking part in the prayers and in the singing, or above all by the common offering of the Sacrifice and by participating together at the Lord's table. This unity is beautifully apparent from the gestures and bodily postures observed together by the faithful.

97.   The faithful, moreover, should not refuse to serve the People of God in gladness whenever they are asked to perform some particular service or function in the celebration.

III. PARTICULAR MINISTRIES

The Ministry of the Instituted Acolyte and Lector

98.   The acolyte is instituted for service at the altar and to assist the Priest and Deacon. It is his place principally to prepare

---

[83] Cf. Second Ecumenical Council of the Vatican, Constitution on the Sacred Liturgy, *Sacrosanctum Concilium*, no. 48; Sacred Congregation of Rites, Instruction, *Eucharisticum mysterium*, 25 May 1967, no. 12: *Acta Apostolicae Sedis* 59 (1967), pp. 548-549.

the altar and the sacred vessels and, if necessary, to distribute the Eucharist to the faithful as an extraordinary minister.[84]

In the ministry of the altar, the acolyte has his own proper functions (*cf. nos. 187-193*), which he must carry out in person.

99.   The lector is instituted to proclaim the readings from Sacred Scripture, with the exception of the Gospel. He may also announce the intentions for the Universal Prayer and, in the absence of a psalmist, recite the Psalm between the readings.

In the celebration of the Eucharist, the lector has his own proper function (*cf. nos. 194-198*), which he himself must carry out.

Other Functions

100. In the absence of an instituted acolyte, there may be deputed lay ministers to serve at the altar and assist the Priest and the Deacon; these carry the cross, the candles, the thurible, the bread, the wine, and the water, or who are even deputed to distribute Holy Communion as extraordinary ministers.[85]

101. In the absence of an instituted lector, other lay people may be deputed to proclaim the readings from Sacred Scripture, people who are truly suited to carrying out this function and carefully prepared, so that by their hearing the readings from the sacred texts the faithful may conceive in their hearts a sweet and living affection for Sacred Scripture.[86]

102. It is the psalmist's place to sing the Psalm or other biblical canticle to be found between the readings. To carry out this function correctly, it is necessary for the psalmist to be

---

[84]   Cf. Code of Canon Law, *Codex Iuris Canonici*, can. 910 § 2; cf. also the Interdicasterial Instruction on certain questions regarding the collaboration of the non-ordained faithful in the sacred ministry of Priests, *Ecclesiae de mysterio*, 15 August 1997, art. 8: *Acta Apostolicae Sedis* 89 (1997), p. 871.

[85]   Cf. Sacred Congregation for the Discipline of the Sacraments, Instruction, *Immensae caritatis*, 29 January 1973, no. 1: *Acta Apostolicae Sedis* 65 (1973), pp. 265-266; Code of Canon Law, *Codex Iuris Canonici*, can. 230 § 3.

[86]   Cf. Second Ecumenical Council of the Vatican, Constitution on the Sacred Liturgy, *Sacrosanctum Concilium*, no. 24.

accomplished in the art of singing Psalms and have a facility in public speaking and elocution.

103. Among the faithful, the *schola cantorum* or choir exercises its own liturgical function, its place being to take care that the parts proper to it, in keeping with the different genres of chant, are properly carried out and to foster the active participation of the faithful by means of the singing.[87] What is said about the *schola cantorum* also applies, with due regard for the relevant norms, to other musicians, and especially the organist.

104. It is fitting that there be a cantor or a choir director to direct and support the people's singing. Indeed, when there is no choir, it is up to the cantor to direct the different chants, with the people taking the part proper to them.[88]

105. A liturgical function is also exercised by:

a) The sacristan, who diligently arranges the liturgical books, the vestments and other things that are necessary for the celebration of Mass.

b) The commentator, who, if appropriate, provides the faithful briefly with explanations and exhortations so as to direct their attention to the celebration and ensure that they are better disposed for understanding it. The commentator's remarks should be thoroughly prepared and notable for their restraint. In performing this function the commentator stands in a suitable place within sight of the faithful, but not at the ambo.

c) Those who take up the collections in the church.

d) Those who, in some regions, welcome the faithful at the church doors, seat them appropriately, and marshal them in processions.

106. It is desirable, at least in cathedrals and in larger churches, to have some competent minister or master of ceremonies, to see to the appropriate arrangement of sacred actions and to

---

[87] Cf. Sacred Congregation of Rites, Instruction, *Musicam sacram*, 5 March 1967, no. 19: *Acta Apostolicae Sedis* 59 (1967), p. 306.

[88] Cf. *ibidem*, no. 21: *Acta Apostolicae Sedis* 59 (1967), pp. 306-307.

their being carried out by the sacred ministers and lay faithful with decorum, order and devotion.

107. Liturgical functions that are not proper to the Priest or the Deacon and are mentioned above (*nos. 100-106*) may even be entrusted by means of a liturgical blessing or a temporary deputation to suitable lay persons chosen by the pastor or the rector of the church.[89] As to the function of serving the Priest at the altar, the norms established by the Bishop for his diocese should be observed.

IV. THE DISTRIBUTION OF FUNCTIONS AND THE PREPARATION OF THE CELEBRATION

108. One and the same Priest must always exercise the presidential function in all of its parts, except for those parts which are proper to a Mass at which the Bishop is present (*cf. above no. 92*).

109. If there are several present who are able to exercise the same ministry, nothing forbids their distributing among themselves and performing different parts of the same ministry or duty. For example, one Deacon may be assigned to execute the sung parts, another to serve at the altar; if there are several readings, it is well to distribute them among a number of readers, and the same applies for other matters. However, it is not at all appropriate that several persons divide a single element of the celebration among themselves, e.g., that the same reading be proclaimed by two readers, one after the other, with the exception of the Passion of the Lord.

110. If at a Mass with the people only one minister is present, that minister may exercise several different functions.

111. There should be harmony and diligence among all those involved in the effective preparation of each liturgical

---

[89] Cf. Pontifical Council for the Interpretation of Legislative Texts, response to *dubium* regarding can. 230 § 2: *Acta Apostolicae Sedis* 86 (1994), p. 541.

celebration in accordance with the Missal and other liturgical books, both as regards the rites and as regards the pastoral and musical aspects. This should take place under the direction of the rector of the church and after consultation with the faithful in things that directly pertain to them. However, the Priest who presides at the celebration always retains the right of arranging those things that pertain to him.[90]

---

[90] Cf. Second Ecumenical Council of the Vatican, Constitution on the Liturgy, *Sacrosanctum Concilium*, no. 22.

Chapter IV

THE DIFFERENT FORMS OF CELEBRATING MASS

112. In the local Church, first place should certainly be given, because of its significance, to the Mass at which the Bishop presides, surrounded by his Presbyterate, Deacons, and lay ministers,[91] and in which the holy People of God participate fully and actively, for it is there that the principal manifestation of the Church is found.

At a Mass celebrated by the Bishop or at which he presides without celebrating the Eucharist, the norms found in the *Caeremoniale Episcoporum* (*Ceremonial of Bishops*) should be observed.[92]

113. Great importance should also be given to a Mass celebrated with any community, but especially with the parish community, inasmuch as it represents the universal Church at a given time and place, and chiefly in the common Sunday celebration.[93]

114. Moreover, among those Masses celebrated by some communities, a particular place belongs to the Conventual Mass, which is a part of the daily Office, or the 'community' Mass. Although such Masses do not involve any special form of celebration, it is nevertheless most fitting that they be celebrated with singing, especially with the full participation of all members of the community, whether of religious or of canons. Therefore, in these Masses all should exercise their function according to the Order or ministry they have received. Hence, it is desirable that all the Priests who are not obliged to celebrate individually

---

[91] Cf. Second Ecumenical Council of the Vatican, Constitution on the Sacred Liturgy, *Sacrosanctum Concilium*, no. 41.

[92] Cf. *Caeremoniale Episcoporum, editio typica*, 1984, nos. 119-186.

[93] Cf. Second Ecumenical Council of the Vatican, Constitution on the Sacred Liturgy, *Sacrosanctum Concilium*, no. 42; Dogmatic Constitution on the Church, *Lumen gentium*, no. 28; Decree on the Ministry and Life of Priests, *Presbyterorum ordinis*, no. 5; Sacred Congregation of Rites, Instruction, *Eucharisticum mysterium*, 25 May 1967, no. 26: *Acta Apostolicae Sedis* 59 (1967), p. 555.

for the pastoral benefit of the faithful concelebrate insofar as possible at the conventual or community Mass. In addition, all Priests belonging to the community who are obliged, as a matter of duty, to celebrate individually for the pastoral benefit of the faithful may also on the same day concelebrate at the conventual or community Mass.[94] For it is preferable that Priests who are present at a celebration of the Eucharist, unless excused for a just reason, should usually exercise the function proper to their Order and hence take part as concelebrants, wearing sacred vestments. Otherwise, they wear their proper choir dress or a surplice over a cassock.

I. MASS WITH THE PEOPLE

115. By Mass with the people is meant a Mass celebrated with the participation of the faithful. Moreover, it is appropriate, insofar as possible, and especially on Sundays and Holydays of Obligation, that the celebration take place with singing and with a suitable number of ministers.[95] It may, however, take place even without singing and with only one minister.

116. If at any celebration of Mass a Deacon is present, he should exercise his function. Furthermore, it is desirable that an acolyte, a reader, and a cantor should usually be there to assist the Priest Celebrant. Indeed, the rite described below foresees an even greater number of ministers.

Things to Be Prepared

117. The altar is to be covered with at least one white cloth. In addition, on or next to the altar are to be placed candlesticks with lighted candles: at least two in any celebration, or even four or six, especially for a Sunday Mass or a Holyday of Obligation, or

---

[94] Cf. Sacred Congregation of Rites, Instruction, *Eucharisticum mysterium*, 25 May 1967, no. 47: *Acta Apostolicae Sedis* 59 (1967), p. 565.

[95] Cf. Sacred Congregation of Rites, Instruction, *Eucharisticum mysterium*, 25 May 1967, no. 26: *Acta Apostolicae Sedis* 59 (1967), p. 555; Instruction, *Musicam sacram*, 5 March 1967, nos. 16, 27: *Acta Apostolicae Sedis* 59 (1967), pp. 305, 308.

if the Diocesan Bishop celebrates, then seven candlesticks with lighted candles. Likewise, on the altar or close to it, there is to be a cross adorned with a figure of Christ crucified. The candles and the cross with the figure of Christ crucified may also be carried in the procession at the Entrance. On the altar itself may be placed a Book of the Gospels distinct from the book of other readings, unless it is carried in the Entrance Procession.

118. Likewise these should be prepared:

a) next to the Priest's chair: the Missal and, if appropriate, a hymnal;

b) at the ambo: the Lectionary;

c) on the credence table: the chalice, corporal, purificator, and, if appropriate, the pall; the paten and, if needed, ciboria; bread for the Communion of the Priest who presides, the Deacon, the ministers, and the people; cruets containing the wine and the water, unless all of these are presented by the faithful in the procession at the Offertory; the vessel of water to be blessed, if the sprinkling of holy water takes place; the Communion-plate for the Communion of the faithful; and whatever is needed for the washing of hands.

It is a praiseworthy practice for the chalice to be covered with a veil, which may be either of the colour of the day or white.

119. In the sacristy, according to the various forms of celebration, there should be prepared the sacred vestments (*cf. nos. 337–341*) for the Priest, the Deacon, and other ministers:

a) for the Priest: the alb, the stole, and the chasuble;

b) for the Deacon: the alb, the stole, and the dalmatic; the latter may be omitted, however, either out of necessity or on account of a lesser degree of solemnity;

c) for the other ministers: albs or other lawfully approved attire.[96]

---

[96] Cf. Interdicasterial Instruction on certain questions regarding the collaboration of the non-ordained faithful in the sacred ministry of Priests, *Ecclesiae de mysterio*, 15 August 1997, art. 6: *Acta Apostolicae Sedis* 89 (1997), p. 869.

All who wear an alb should use a cincture and an amice unless, due to the form of the alb, they are not needed.

When the Entrance takes place with a procession, the following are also to be prepared: a Book of the Gospels; on Sundays and festive days, a thurible and incense boat, if incense is being used; the cross to be carried in procession; and candlesticks with lighted candles.

A) MASS WITHOUT A DEACON

The Introductory Rites

120. When the people are gathered, the Priest and ministers, wearing the sacred vestments, go in procession to the altar in this order:

a) the thurifer carrying a smoking thurible, if incense is being used;

b) ministers who carry lighted candles, and between them an acolyte or other minister with the cross;

c) the acolytes and the other ministers;

d) a reader, who may carry a Book of the Gospels (though not a Lectionary), slightly elevated;

e) the Priest who is to celebrate the Mass.

If incense is being used, before the procession begins, the Priest puts some into the thurible and blesses it with the Sign of the Cross without saying anything.

121. During the procession to the altar, the Entrance Chant takes place (*cf. nos. 47-48*).

122. When they reach the altar, the Priest and ministers make a profound bow.

The cross adorned with a figure of Christ crucified, and carried in procession, may be placed next to the altar to serve as the altar cross, in which case it must be the only cross used; otherwise it is put away in a dignified place. As for the candlesticks, these are placed on the altar or near it. It is a praiseworthy practice for the Book of the Gospels to be placed on the altar.

123. The Priest goes up to the altar and venerates it with a kiss. Then, if appropriate, he incenses the cross and the altar, walking around the latter.

124. Once all this has been done, the Priest goes to the chair. When the Entrance Chant is concluded, with everybody standing, the Priest and faithful sign themselves with the Sign of the Cross. The Priest says: In the name of the Father, and of the Son, and of the Holy Spirit. The people reply, Amen.

Then, facing the people and extending his hands, the Priest greets the people, using one of the formulas indicated. The Priest himself or some other minister may also very briefly introduce the faithful to the Mass of the day.

125. The Penitential Act follows. After this, the Kyrie is sung or said, in accordance with the rubrics (*cf. no. 52*).

126. For celebrations where it is prescribed, the Gloria in excelsis (*Glory to God in the highest*) is either sung or said (*cf. no. 53*).

127. The Priest then calls upon the people to pray, saying, with hands joined, Let us pray. All pray silently with the Priest for a brief time. Then the Priest, with hands extended, says the Collect, at the end of which the people acclaim, Amen.

The Liturgy of the Word

128. After the Collect, all sit. The Priest may, very briefly, introduce the faithful to the Liturgy of the Word. Then the reader goes to the ambo and, from the Lectionary already placed there before Mass, proclaims the First Reading, to which all listen. At the end, the reader pronounces the acclamation The word of the Lord, and all reply, Thanks be to God.

Then a few moments of silence may be observed, if appropriate, so that all may meditate on what they have heard.

129. Then the psalmist or the reader proclaims the verses of the Psalm and the people make the response as usual.

130. If there is to be a Second Reading before the Gospel, the reader proclaims it from the ambo. All listen and at the end reply to the acclamation, as noted above (*no. 128*). Then, if appropriate, a few moments of silence may be observed.

131. After this, all rise, and the Alleluia or other chant is sung as the liturgical time requires (*cf. nos. 62–64*).

132. During the singing of the Alleluia or other chant, if incense is being used, the Priest puts some into the thurible and blesses it. Then, with hands joined, he bows profoundly before the altar and quietly says the prayer Munda cor meum (*Cleanse my heart*).

133. If the Book of the Gospels is on the altar, the Priest then takes it and approaches the ambo, carrying the Book of the Gospels slightly elevated. He is preceded by the lay ministers, who may carry the thurible and the candles. Those present turn towards the ambo as a sign of special reverence for the Gospel of Christ.

134. At the ambo, the Priest opens the book and, with hands joined, says, The Lord be with you, to which the people reply, And with your spirit. Then he says, A reading from the holy Gospel, making the Sign of the Cross with his thumb on the book and on his forehead, mouth, and breast, which everyone else does as well. The people acclaim, Glory to you, O Lord. The Priest incenses the book, if incense is being used (*cf. nos. 276-277*). Then he proclaims the Gospel and at the end pronounces the acclamation The Gospel of the Lord, to which all reply, Praise to you, Lord Jesus Christ. The Priest kisses the book, saying quietly the formula Per evangelica dicta (*Through the words of the Gospel*).

135. If no reader is present, the Priest himself proclaims all the readings and the Psalm, standing at the ambo. If incense is being used, he puts some incense into the thurible at the ambo, blesses it, and, bowing profoundly, says the prayer Munda cor meum (*Cleanse my heart*).

136. The Priest, standing at the chair or at the ambo itself or, if appropriate, in another worthy place, gives the Homily. When the Homily is over, a period of silence may be observed.

137. The Symbol or Creed is sung or recited by the Priest together with the people (*cf. no. 68*) with everyone standing. At the words et incarnatus est, etc. (*and by the Holy Spirit . . . and became man*) all make a profound bow; but on the Solemnities of the Annunciation and of the Nativity of the Lord, all genuflect.

138. After the recitation of the Symbol or Creed, the Priest, standing at the chair with his hands joined, by means of a brief address calls upon the faithful to participate in the Universal Prayer. Then the cantor, the reader, or another person announces the intentions from the ambo or from some other suitable place while facing the people. The latter take their part by replying in supplication. At the very end, the Priest, with hands extended, concludes the petitions with a prayer.

The Liturgy of the Eucharist

139. When the Universal Prayer is over, all sit, and the Offertory Chant begins (*cf. no. 74*).

An acolyte or other lay minister places the corporal, the purificator, the chalice, the pall, and the Missal on the altar.

140. It is desirable that the participation of the faithful be expressed by an offering, whether of bread and wine for the celebration of the Eucharist or of other gifts to relieve the needs of the Church and of the poor.

The offerings of the faithful are received by the Priest, assisted by the acolyte or other minister. The bread and wine for the Eucharist are carried to the Celebrant, who places them on the altar, while other gifts are put in another suitable place (*cf. no. 73*).

141. The Priest accepts the paten with the bread at the altar, holds it slightly raised above the altar with both hands and says quietly, Benedictus es, Domine (*Blessed are you, Lord God*). Then he places the paten with the bread on the corporal.

142. After this, as the minister presents the cruets, the Priest stands at the side of the altar and pours wine and a little water into the chalice, saying quietly, Per huius aquae (*By the mystery of this water*). He returns to the middle of the altar and with both hands raises the chalice a little, and says quietly, Benedictus es, Domine (*Blessed are you, Lord God*). Then he places the chalice on the corporal and, if appropriate, covers it with a pall.

If, however, there is no Offertory Chant and the organ is not played, in the presentation of the bread and wine the Priest may say the formulas of blessing aloud and the people acclaim, Blessed be God for ever.

143. After placing the chalice on the altar, the Priest bows profoundly and says quietly, In spiritu humilitatis *(With humble spirit*).

144. If incense is being used, the Priest then puts some in the thurible, blesses it without saying anything, and incenses the offerings, the cross, and the altar. While standing at the side of the altar, a minister incenses the Priest and then the people.

145. After the prayer In spiritu humilitatis (*With humble spirit*) or after the incensation, the Priest washes his hands standing at the side of the altar and, as the minister pours the water, says quietly, Lava me, Domine (*Wash me, O Lord*).

146. Returning to the middle of the altar, and standing facing the people, the Priest extends and then joins his hands, and calls upon the people to pray, saying, Orate, fratres (*Pray, brethren*). The people rise and make the response May the Lord accept the sacrifice, etc. Then the Priest, with hands extended, says the Prayer over the Offerings. At the end the people acclaim, Amen.

147. Then the Priest begins the Eucharistic Prayer. In accordance with the rubrics (*cf. no. 365*), he selects a Eucharistic Prayer from those found in the Roman Missal or approved by the Apostolic See. By its very nature, the Eucharistic Prayer requires that only the Priest say it, in virtue of his Ordination. The people, for their part, should associate themselves with the Priest in faith and in silence, as well as by means of their interventions as prescribed in the course of the Eucharistic Prayer: namely, the responses in the Preface dialogue, the Sanctus (*Holy, Holy, Holy*), the acclamation after the Consecration, the acclamation Amen after the concluding doxology, as well as other acclamations approved by the Conference of Bishops with the *recognitio* of the Holy See.

It is most appropriate that the Priest sing those parts of the Eucharistic Prayer for which musical notation is provided.

148. As he begins the Eucharistic Prayer, the Priest extends his hands and sings or says, The Lord be with you. The people reply, And with your spirit. As he continues, saying, Lift up your hearts, he raises his hands. The people reply, We lift them up to the Lord. Then the Priest, with hands extended, adds, Let us give thanks to the Lord our God, and the people reply, It is right and just. After this, the Priest, with hands extended, continues the Preface. At its conclusion, he joins his hands and, together with all those present, sings or says aloud the Sanctus (*Holy, Holy, Holy*) (*cf. no. 79 b*).

149. The Priest continues the Eucharistic Prayer in accordance with the rubrics that are set out in each of the Prayers.

If the celebrant is a Bishop, in the Prayers, after the words N., our Pope, he adds, and me, your unworthy servant. If, however, the Bishop is celebrating outside his own diocese, after the words with . . . N., our Pope, he adds, my brother N., the Bishop of this Church, and me, your unworthy servant; or after the words especially . . . N., our Pope, he adds, my brother N., the Bishop of this Church, and me, your unworthy servant.

The Diocesan Bishop, or one who is equivalent to the Diocesan Bishop in law, must be mentioned by means of this formula: together with your servant N., our Pope, and N., our Bishop (or Vicar, Prelate, Prefect, Abbot).

It is permitted to mention Coadjutor Bishop and Auxiliary Bishops in the Eucharistic Prayer, but not other Bishops who happen to be present. When several are to be mentioned, this is done with the collective formula: N., our Bishop and his assistant Bishops.

In each of the Eucharistic Prayers, these formulas are to be adapted according to the requirements of grammar.

150. A little before the Consecration, if appropriate, a minister rings a small bell as a signal to the faithful. The minister also rings the small bell at each elevation by the Priest, according to local custom.

If incense is being used, when the host and the chalice are shown to the people after the Consecration, a minister incenses them.

151. After the Consecration when the Priest has said, The mystery of faith, the people pronounce the acclamation, using one of the prescribed formulas.

At the end of the Eucharistic Prayer, the Priest takes the paten with the host and the chalice and elevates them both while pronouncing alone the doxology Through him. At the end the people acclaim, Amen. After this, the Priest places the paten and the chalice on the corporal.

152. After the Eucharistic Prayer is concluded, the Priest, with hands joined, says alone the introduction to the Lord's Prayer, and then with hands extended, he pronounces the prayer together with the people.

153. After the Lord's Prayer is concluded, the Priest, with hands extended, says alone the embolism Libera nos (*Deliver us, Lord*). At the end, the people acclaim, For the kingdom.

154. Then the Priest, with hands extended, says aloud the prayer Domine Iesu Christe, qui dixisti (*Lord Jesus Christ, who said to your Apostles*) and when it is concluded, extending and then

joining his hands, he announces the greeting of peace, facing the people and saying, The peace of the Lord be with you always. The people reply, And with your spirit. After this, if appropriate, the Priest adds, Let us offer each other the sign of peace.

The Priest may give the Sign of Peace to the ministers but always remains within the sanctuary, so that the celebration is not disrupted. He may do the same if, for a reasonable cause, he wishes to offer the Sign of Peace to a small number of the faithful. According to what is decided by the Conference of Bishops, all express to one another peace, communion, and charity. While the Sign of Peace is being given, it is permissible to say, The peace of the Lord be with you always, to which the reply is Amen.

155. After this, the Priest takes the host, breaks it over the paten, and places a small piece in the chalice, saying quietly, Haec commixtio (*May this mingling*). Meanwhile the Agnus Dei (*Lamb of God*) is sung or said by the choir and by the people (*cf. no. 83*).

156. Then the Priest, with hands joined, says quietly the prayer for Communion, either Domine Iesu Christe, Fili Dei vivi (*Lord Jesus Christ, Son of the living God*) or Perceptio Corporis et Sanguinis tui (*May the receiving of your Body and Blood*).

157. When the prayer is concluded, the Priest genuflects, takes a host consecrated at the same Mass, and, holding it slightly raised above the paten or above the chalice, facing the people, says, Ecce Agnus Dei (*Behold the Lamb of God*) and together with the people he adds, Lord, I am not worthy.

158. After this, standing facing the altar, the Priest says quietly, Corpus Christi custodiat me in vitam aeternam (*May the Body of Christ keep me safe for eternal life*), and reverently consumes the Body of Christ. Then he takes the chalice, saying quietly, Sanguis Christi custodiat me in vitam aeternam (*May the Blood of Christ keep me safe for eternal life*), and reverently partakes of the Blood of Christ.

159. While the Priest is receiving the Sacrament, the Communion Chant begins (*cf. no. 86*).

160. The Priest then takes the paten or ciborium and approaches the communicants, who usually come up in procession.

It is not permitted for the faithful to take the consecrated Bread or the sacred chalice by themselves and, still less, to hand them on from one to another among themselves. The faithful communicate either kneeling or standing, as has been determined by the norms of the Conference of Bishops. However, when they communicate standing, it is recommended that before receiving the Sacrament they make an appropriate sign of reverence, to be determined in the same norms.

In England and Wales, and in Scotland: The Priest then takes the paten or ciborium and approaches the communicants, who usually come up in procession.

It is not permitted for the faithful to take the consecrated Bread or the sacred chalice by themselves and, still less, to hand them on from one to another among themselves. In the Dioceses of England and Wales, and of Scotland Holy Communion is to be received standing, though individual members of the faithful may choose to receive Communion while kneeling. However, when they communicate standing, it is recommended that the faithful bow in reverence before receiving the Sacrament.

---

161. If Communion is given only under the species of bread, the Priest raises the host slightly and shows it to each, saying, The Body of Christ. The communicant replies, Amen, and receives the Sacrament either on the tongue or, where this is allowed, in the hand, the choice lying with the communicant. As soon as the communicant receives the host, he or she consumes the whole of it.

If, however, Communion is given under both kinds, the rite prescribed in nos. 284-287 is to be followed.

162. In the distribution of Communion the Priest may be assisted by other Priests who happen to be present. If such Priests are not present and there is a truly large number of communicants, the Priest may call upon extraordinary ministers to assist him, that is, duly instituted acolytes or even other faithful who have been duly deputed for this purpose.[97] In case of necessity, the Priest may depute suitable faithful for this single occasion.[98]

These ministers should not approach the altar before the Priest has received Communion, and they are always to receive from the hands of the Priest Celebrant the vessel containing the species of the Most Holy Eucharist for distribution to the faithful.

163. When the distribution of Communion is over, the Priest himself immediately and completely consumes at the altar any consecrated wine that happens to remain; as for any consecrated hosts that are left, he either consumes them at the altar or carries them to the place designated for the reservation of the Eucharist.

Upon returning to the altar, the Priest collects the fragments, should any remain, and he stands at the altar or at the credence table and purifies the paten or ciborium over the chalice, and after this purifies the chalice, saying quietly the formula Quod ore sumpsimus, Domine (*What has passed our lips*), and dries the chalice with a purificator. If the vessels are purified at the altar, they are carried to the credence table by a minister. Nevertheless, it is also permitted to leave vessels needing to be purified, especially if there are several, on a corporal, suitably covered, either on the altar or on the credence table, and to purify them immediately after Mass, after the Dismissal of the people.

---

[97] Cf. Sacred Congregation for the Sacraments and Divine Worship, Instruction, *Inaestimabile donum*, 3 April 1980, no. 10: *Acta Apostolicae Sedis* 72 (1980), p. 336; Interdicasterial Instruction on certain questions regarding the collaboration of the non-ordained faithful in the sacred ministry of Priests, *Ecclesiae de mysterio*, 15 August 1997, art. 8: *Acta Apostolicae Sedis* 89 (1997), p. 871.

[98] Cf. Roman Missal, Appendix III, Rite of Deputing a Minister to Distribute Holy Communion on a Single Occasion, p. 1511.

164. After this, the Priest may return to the chair. A sacred silence may now be observed for some time, or a Psalm or other canticle of praise or a hymn may be sung (*cf. no. 88*).

165. Then, standing at the chair or at the altar, and facing the people with hands joined, the Priest says, Let us pray; then, with hands extended, he recites the Prayer after Communion. A brief period of silence may precede the prayer, unless this has been already observed immediately after Communion. At the end of the prayer the people acclaim, Amen.

The Concluding Rites

166. When the Prayer after Communion is concluded, brief announcements should be made to the people, if there are any.

167. Then the Priest, extending his hands, greets the people, saying, The Lord be with you. They reply, And with your spirit. The Priest, joining his hands again and then immediately placing his left hand on his breast, raises his right hand and adds, May almighty God bless you and, as he makes the Sign of the Cross over the people, he continues, the Father, and the Son, and the Holy Spirit. All reply, Amen.

On certain days and occasions this blessing, in accordance with the rubrics, is expanded and expressed by a Prayer over the People or another more solemn formula.

A Bishop blesses the people with the appropriate formula, making the Sign of the Cross three times over the people.[99]

168. Immediately after the Blessing, with hands joined, the Priest adds, Ite, missa est (*Go forth, the Mass is ended*) and all reply, Thanks be to God.

169. Then the Priest venerates the altar as usual with a kiss and, after making a profound bow with the lay ministers, he withdraws with them.

---

[99] Cf. *Caeremoniale Episcoporum*, editio typica, 1984, nos. 1118-1121.

170. If, however, another liturgical action follows the Mass, the Concluding Rites, that is, the Greeting, the Blessing, and the Dismissal, are omitted.

B) Mass with a Deacon

171. When he is present at the celebration of the Eucharist, a Deacon should exercise his ministry, wearing sacred vestments. In fact, the Deacon:

a) assists the Priest and walks at his side;

b) ministers at the altar, both as regards the chalice and the book;

c) proclaims the Gospel and may, at the direction of the Priest Celebrant, give the Homily (*cf. no. 66*);

d) guides the faithful people by giving appropriate instructions, and announces the intentions of the Universal Prayer;

e) assists the Priest Celebrant in distributing Communion, and purifies and arranges the sacred vessels;

f) carries out the duties of other ministers himself, if necessary, when none of them is present.

The Introductory Rites

172. Carrying the Book of the Gospels slightly elevated, the Deacon precedes the Priest as he approaches the altar or else walks at the Priest's side.

173. When he reaches the altar, if he is carrying the Book of the Gospels, he omits the sign of reverence and goes up to the altar. It is a praiseworthy practice for him to place the Book of the Gospels on the altar, after which, together with the Priest, he venerates the altar with a kiss.

If, however, he is not carrying the Book of the Gospels, he makes a profound bow to the altar with the Priest in the customary way and with him venerates the altar with a kiss.

Lastly, if incense is being used, he assists the Priest in putting some into the thurible and in incensing the cross and the altar.

174. Once the altar has been incensed, the Deacon goes to the chair together with the Priest and there stands at the Priest's side and assists him as necessary.

The Liturgy of the Word

175. During the singing of the Alleluia or other chant, if incense is being used, the Deacon ministers to the Priest as he puts incense into the thurible. Then, bowing profoundly before the Priest, he asks for the blessing, saying in a low voice, Your blessing, Father. The Priest blesses him, saying, May the Lord be in your heart. The Deacon signs himself with the Sign of the Cross and replies, Amen. Having bowed to the altar, he then takes up the Book of the Gospels which was placed on it and proceeds to the ambo, carrying the book slightly elevated. He is preceded by a thurifer carrying a smoking thurible and by ministers with lighted candles. At the ambo the Deacon greets the people, with hands joined, saying, The Lord be with you. After this, at the words A reading from the holy Gospel, he signs with his thumb the book and then himself on his forehead, mouth, and breast. He incenses the book and proclaims the Gospel reading. When this is done, he acclaims, The Gospel of the Lord, and all reply, Praise to you, Lord Jesus Christ. He then venerates the book with a kiss, saying quietly the formula Per evangelica dicta (*Through the words of the Gospel*), and returns to the Priest's side.

When the Deacon is assisting the Bishop, he carries the book to him to be kissed, or else kisses it himself, saying quietly the formula Per evangelica dicta (*Through the words of the Gospel*). In more solemn celebrations, if appropriate, the Bishop may impart a blessing to the people with the Book of the Gospels.

Lastly, the Deacon may carry the Book of the Gospels to the credence table or to another suitable and dignified place.

176. Moreover, if there is no other suitable reader present, the Deacon should proclaim the other readings as well.

177. After the introduction by the Priest, it is the Deacon himself who announces the intentions of the Universal Prayer, usually from the ambo.

The Liturgy of the Eucharist

178. After the Universal Prayer, while the Priest remains at the chair, the Deacon prepares the altar, assisted by the acolyte, but it is the Deacon's place to take care of the sacred vessels himself. He also assists the Priest in receiving the people's gifts. After this, he hands the Priest the paten with the bread to be consecrated, pours wine and a little water into the chalice, saying quietly, By the mystery of this water, etc. and after this presents the chalice to the Priest. He may also carry out the preparation of the chalice at the credence table. If incense is being used, the Deacon assists the Priest during the incensation of the offerings, the cross, and the altar; and after this the Deacon himself or the acolyte incenses the Priest and the people.

179. During the Eucharistic Prayer, the Deacon stands near the Priest, but slightly behind him, so that when necessary he may assist the Priest with the chalice or the Missal.

From the epiclesis until the Priest shows the chalice, the Deacon usually remains kneeling. If several Deacons are present, one of them may place incense in the thurible for the Consecration and incense the host and the chalice at the elevation.

180. At the concluding doxology of the Eucharistic Prayer, the Deacon stands next to the Priest, and holds the chalice elevated while the Priest elevates the paten with the host, until the people have acclaimed, Amen.

181. After the Priest has said the prayer for the Rite of Peace and the greeting The peace of the Lord be with you always and the people have replied, And with your spirit, the Deacon,

if appropriate, says the invitation to the Sign of Peace. With hands joined, he faces the people and says, Let us offer each other the sign of peace. Then he himself receives the Sign of Peace from the Priest and may offer it to those other ministers who are nearest to him.

182. After the Priest's Communion, the Deacon receives Communion under both kinds from the Priest himself and then assists the Priest in distributing Communion to the people. If Communion is given under both kinds, the Deacon himself administers the chalice to the communicants; and, when the distribution is over, standing at the altar, he immediately and reverently consumes all of the Blood of Christ that remains, assisted, if the case requires, by other Deacons and Priests.

183. When the distribution of Communion is over, the Deacon returns to the altar with the Priest, collects the fragments, should any remain, and then carries the chalice and other sacred vessels to the credence table, where he purifies them and arranges them as usual, while the Priest returns to the chair. Nevertheless, it is also permitted to leave vessels needing to be purified on a corporal, suitably covered, on the credence table, and to purify them immediately after Mass, following the Dismissal of the people.

The Concluding Rites

184. Once the Prayer after Communion has been said, the Deacon makes brief announcements to the people, if indeed any need to be made, unless the Priest prefers to do this himself.

185. If a Prayer over the People or a formula of Solemn Blessing is used, the Deacon says, Bow down for the blessing. After the Priest's blessing, the Deacon, with hands joined and facing the people, dismisses the people, saying, Ite, missa est (*Go forth, the Mass is ended*).

186. Then, together with the Priest, the Deacon venerates the altar with a kiss, makes a profound bow, and withdraws in a manner similar to the Entrance Procession.

C) The Functions of the Acolyte

187. The functions that the acolyte may carry out are of various kinds and several may occur at the same moment. Hence, it is desirable that these duties be suitably distributed among several acolytes. If, in fact, only one acolyte is present, he should perform the more important duties while the rest are to be distributed among several ministers.

The Introductory Rites

188. In the procession to the altar, the acolyte may carry the cross, walking between two ministers with lighted candles. Upon reaching the altar, however, the acolyte places the cross upright near the altar so that it may serve as the altar cross; otherwise, he puts it away in a dignified place. Then he takes his place in the sanctuary.

189. Through the entire celebration, it is for the acolyte to approach the Priest or the Deacon, whenever necessary, in order to present the book to them and to assist them in any other way required. Thus it is appropriate that, insofar as possible, the acolyte should occupy a place from which he can easily carry out his ministry either at the chair or at the altar.

The Liturgy of the Eucharist

190. In the absence of a Deacon, after the Universal Prayer and while the Priest remains at the chair, the acolyte places the corporal, the purificator, the chalice, the pall, and the Missal on the altar. Then, if necessary, the acolyte assists the Priest in receiving the gifts of the people and, if appropriate, brings the bread and wine to the altar and hands them to the Priest. If incense is being used, the acolyte presents the thurible to the Priest and assists him while he incenses the offerings, the cross, and the altar. Then the acolyte incenses the Priest and the people.

191. A duly instituted acolyte, as an extraordinary minister, may, if necessary, assist the Priest in distributing Communion to the people.[100] If Communion is given under both kinds, in the absence of a Deacon, the acolyte administers the chalice to the communicants or holds the chalice if Communion is given by intinction.

192. Likewise, after the distribution of Communion is complete, a duly instituted acolyte helps the Priest or Deacon to purify and arrange the sacred vessels. In the absence of a Deacon, a duly instituted acolyte carries the sacred vessels to the credence table and there purifies them, wipes them and arranges them as usual.

193. After the celebration of Mass, the acolyte and other ministers return together with the Deacon and the Priest in procession to the sacristy, in the same manner and in the same order in which they entered.

D) The Functions of the Reader

Introductory Rites

194. In the procession to the altar, in the absence of a Deacon, the reader, wearing approved attire, may carry the Book of the Gospels, slightly elevated. In that case, the reader walks in front of the Priest but otherwise walks along with the other ministers.

195. Upon reaching the altar, the reader makes a profound bow with the others. If he is carrying the Book of the Gospels, he approaches the altar and places the Book of the Gospels upon it. Then the reader takes his own place in the sanctuary with the other ministers.

---

[100] Paul VI, Apostolic Letter, *Ministeria quaedam*, 15 August 1972: *Acta Apostolicae Sedis* 64 (1972), p. 532.

The Liturgy of the Word

196. The reader reads from the ambo the readings that precede the Gospel. In the absence of a psalmist, the reader may also proclaim the Responsorial Psalm after the First Reading.

197. In the absence of a Deacon, the reader, after the introduction by the Priest, may announce the intentions of the Universal Prayer from the ambo.

198. If there is no singing at the Entrance or at Communion and the antiphons given in the Missal are not recited by the faithful, the reader may read them at an appropriate time (*cf. nos. 48, 87*).

II. CONCELEBRATED MASS

199. Concelebration, by which the unity of the Priesthood, of the Sacrifice, and also of the whole People of God is appropriately expressed, is prescribed by the rite itself for the Ordination of a Bishop and of Priests, at the Blessing of an Abbot, and at the Chrism Mass.

It is recommended, moreover, unless the good of the Christian faithful requires or suggests otherwise, at:

a) the Evening Mass of the Lord's Supper;

b) the Mass during Councils, gatherings of Bishops, and Synods;

c) the Conventual Mass and the principal Mass in churches and oratories;

d) Masses at any kind of gathering of Priests, either secular or religious.[101]

Every Priest, however, is allowed to celebrate the Eucharist individually, though not at the same time as a concelebration is taking place in the same church or oratory. However, on

---

[101] Cf. Second Ecumenical Council of the Vatican, Constitution on the Sacred Liturgy, *Sacrosanctum Concilium*, no. 57; Code of Canon Law, *Codex Iuris Canonici*, can. 902.

Holy Thursday, and for the Mass of the Easter Vigil, it is not permitted to celebrate Mass individually.

200. Visiting Priests should be gladly admitted to concelebration of the Eucharist, provided their priestly standing has been ascertained.

201. When there is a large number of Priests, concelebration may take place even several times on the same day, where necessity or pastoral advantage commend it. However, this must be done at different times or in distinct sacred places.[102]

202. It is for the Bishop, in accordance with the norm of law, to regulate the discipline for concelebration in all churches and oratories of his diocese.

203. To be held in particularly high regard is that concelebration in which the Priests of any given diocese concelebrate with their own Bishop at a stational Mass, especially on the more solemn days of the liturgical year, at the Ordination Mass of a new Bishop of the diocese or of his Coadjutor or Auxiliary, at the Chrism Mass, at the Evening Mass of the Lord's Supper, at celebrations of the Founder Saint of a local Church or the Patron of the diocese, on anniversaries of the Bishop, and, lastly, on the occasion of a Synod or a pastoral visitation.

In the same way, concelebration is recommended whenever Priests gather together with their own Bishop whether on the occasion of a retreat or at any other gathering. In these cases the sign of the unity of the priesthood and also of the Church inherent in every concelebration is made more clearly manifest.[103]

204. For a particular reason, having to do either with the significance of the rite or of the festivity, the faculty is given to

---

[102] Cf. Sacred Congregation of Rites, Instruction, *Eucharisticum mysterium*, 25 May 1967, no. 47: *Acta Apostolicae Sedis* 59 (1967), p. 566.

[103] Cf. *ibidem*, no. 47: p. 565.

celebrate or concelebrate more than once on the same day in the following cases:

a) a Priest who has celebrated or concelebrated the Chrism Mass on Thursday of Holy Week may also celebrate or concelebrate the Evening Mass of the Lord's Supper;

b) a Priest who has celebrated or concelebrated the Mass of the Easter Vigil may celebrate or concelebrate Mass during the day on Easter Sunday;

c) on the Nativity of the Lord (Christmas Day), all Priests may celebrate or concelebrate three Masses, provided the Masses are celebrated at their proper times of day;

d) on the Commemoration of All the Faithful Departed (All Souls' Day), all Priests may celebrate or concelebrate three Masses, provided that the celebrations take place at different times, and with due regard for what has been laid down regarding the application of second and third Masses;[104]

e) a Priest who concelebrates with the Bishop or his delegate at a Synod or pastoral visitation, or concelebrates on the occasion of a gathering of Priests, may celebrate Mass again for the benefit of the faithful. This holds also, with due regard for the prescriptions of law, for groups of religious.

205. A concelebrated Mass, whatever its form, is arranged in accordance with the norms commonly in force (*cf. nos. 112– 198*), observing or adapting however what is set out below.

206. No one is ever to join a concelebration or to be admitted as a concelebrant once the Mass has already begun.

207. In the sanctuary there should be prepared:

a) seats and texts for the concelebrating Priests;

b) on the credence table: a chalice of sufficient size or else several chalices.

---

[104] Cf. Benedict XV, Apostolic Constitution, *Incruentum altaris sacrificium*, 10 August 1915: *Acta Apostolicae Sedis* 7 (1915), pp. 401-404.

208. If a Deacon is not present, the functions proper to him are to be carried out by some of the concelebrants.

If other ministers are also absent, their proper parts may be entrusted to other suitable faithful laypeople; otherwise, they are carried out by some of the concelebrants.

209. The concelebrants put on in the vesting room, or other suitable place, the sacred vestments they customarily wear when celebrating Mass individually. However, should a just cause arise (e.g., a more considerable number of concelebrants or a lack of vestments), concelebrants other than the principal celebrant may omit the chasuble and simply wear the stole over the alb.

The Introductory Rites

210. When everything has been properly arranged, the procession moves as usual through the church to the altar. The concelebrating Priests walk ahead of the principal celebrant.

211. On arriving at the altar, the concelebrants and the principal celebrant, after making a profound bow, venerate the altar with a kiss, then go to their designated seats. As for the principal celebrant, if appropriate, he incenses the cross and the altar and then goes to the chair.

The Liturgy of the Word

212. During the Liturgy of the Word, the concelebrants remain at their places, sitting or standing whenever the principal celebrant does.

When the Alleluia is begun, all rise, except for a Bishop, who puts incense into the thurible without saying anything and blesses the Deacon or, in the absence of a Deacon, the concelebrant who is to proclaim the Gospel. However, in a concelebration where a Priest presides, the concelebrant who in the absence of a Deacon proclaims the Gospel neither requests nor receives the blessing of the principal celebrant.

213. The Homily is usually given by the principal celebrant or by one of the concelebrants.

The Liturgy of the Eucharist

214. The Preparation of the Gifts (*cf. nos. 139-146*) is carried out by the principal celebrant, while the other concelebrants remain at their places.

215. After the Prayer over the Offerings has been said by the principal celebrant, the concelebrants approach the altar and stand around it, but in such a way that they do not obstruct the execution of the rites and that the sacred action may be seen clearly by the faithful. Nor should they obstruct the Deacon whenever he needs to approach the altar by reason of his ministry.

The Deacon exercises his ministry near the altar, assisting whenever necessary with the chalice and the Missal. However, insofar as possible, he stands back slightly, behind the concelebrating Priests standing around the principal celebrant.

The Manner of Pronouncing the Eucharistic Prayer

216. The Preface is sung or said by the principal Priest Celebrant alone; but the Sanctus (*Holy, Holy, Holy*) is sung or recited by all the concelebrants, together with the people and the choir.

217. After the Sanctus (*Holy, Holy, Holy*), the concelebrating Priests continue the Eucharistic Prayer in the way described below. Only the principal celebrant makes the gestures, unless other indications are given.

218. The parts pronounced by all the concelebrants together and especially the words of Consecration, which all are obliged to say, are to be recited in such a manner that the concelebrants speak them in a low voice and that the principal celebrant's voice is heard clearly. In this way the words can be more easily understood by the people.

It is a praiseworthy practice for the parts that are to be said by all the concelebrants together and for which musical notation is provided in the Missal to be sung.

Eucharistic Prayer I, or the Roman Canon

219. In Eucharistic Prayer I, or the Roman Canon, the Te igitur (*To you, therefore, most merciful Father*) is said by the principal celebrant alone, with hands extended.

220. It is appropriate that the commemoration (*Memento*) of the living and the Communicantes (*In communion with those*) be assigned to one or other of the concelebrating Priests, who then pronounces these prayers alone, with hands extended, and in a loud voice.

221. The Hanc igitur (*Therefore, Lord, we pray*) is said once again by the principal celebrant alone, with hands extended.

222. From the Quam oblationem (*Be pleased, O God, we pray*) up to and including the Supplices (*In humble prayer we ask you, almighty God*), the principal celebrant alone makes the gestures, while all the concelebrants pronounce everything together, in this manner:

a) the Quam oblationem (*Be pleased, O God, we pray*) with hands extended toward the offerings;

b) the Qui pridie (*On the day before he was to suffer*), and the Simili modo (*In a similar way*) with hands joined;

c) the words of the Lord, with each extending his right hand toward the bread and toward the chalice, if this seems appropriate; and at the elevation looking toward them and after this bowing profoundly;

d) the Unde et memores (*Therefore, O Lord, as we celebrate the memorial*) and the Supra quae (*Be pleased to look upon*) with hands extended;

e) for the Supplices (*In humble prayer we ask you, almighty God*) up to and including the words through this participation at the altar, bowing with hands joined; then standing upright and crossing themselves at the words may be filled with every grace and heavenly blessing.

223. It is appropriate that the commemoration (*Memento*) of the dead and the Nobis quoque peccatoribus (*To us, also, your servants*) be assigned to one or other of the concelebrants, who pronounces them alone, with hands extended, and in a loud voice.

224. At the words To us, also, your servants, who though sinners, of the Nobis quoque peccatoribus, all the concelebrants strike their breast.

225. The Per quem haec omnia (*Through whom you continue*) is said by the principal celebrant alone.

Eucharistic Prayer II

226. In Eucharistic Prayer II, the part You are indeed Holy, O Lord is pronounced by the principal celebrant alone, with hands extended.

227. In the parts from Make holy, therefore, these gifts to the end of Humbly we pray, all the concelebrants pronounce everything together as follows:

a) the part Make holy, therefore, these gifts, with hands extended toward the offerings;

b) the parts At the time he was betrayed and In a similar way with hands joined;

c) the words of the Lord, with each extending his right hand toward the bread and toward the chalice, if this seems appropriate; and at the elevation looking toward them and after this bowing profoundly;

d) the parts Therefore, as we celebrate and Humbly we pray with hands extended.

228. It is appropriate that the intercessions for the living, Remember, Lord, your Church, and for the dead, Remember also our brothers and sisters, be assigned to one or other of

the concelebrants, who pronounces them alone, with hands extended, and in a loud voice.

Eucharistic Prayer III

229. In Eucharistic Prayer III, the part You are indeed Holy, O Lord is pronounced by the principal celebrant alone, with hands extended.

230. In the parts from Therefore, O Lord, we humbly implore you to the end of Look, we pray upon the oblation, all the concelebrants pronounce everything together as follows:

a) the part Therefore, O Lord, we humbly implore you with hands extended toward the offerings;

b) the parts For on the night he was betrayed and In a similar way with hands joined;

c) the words of the Lord, with each extending his right hand toward the bread and toward the chalice, if this seems appropriate; and at the elevation looking toward them and after this bowing profoundly;

d) the parts Therefore, O Lord, as we celebrate the memorial and Look, we pray, upon the oblation with hands extended.

231. It is appropriate that the intercessions May he make of us an eternal offering to you, and May this Sacrifice of our reconciliation, and To our departed brothers and sisters be assigned to one or other of the concelebrants, who pronounces them alone, with hands extended, and in a loud voice.

Eucharistic Prayer IV

232. In Eucharistic Prayer IV, the part We give you praise, Father most holy up to and including the words he might sanctify creation to the full is pronounced by the principal celebrant alone, with hands extended.

233. In the parts from Therefore, O Lord, we pray to the end of Look, O Lord, upon the Sacrifice, all the concelebrants pronounce everything together as follows:

a) the part Therefore, O Lord, we pray with hands extended toward the offerings;

b) the parts For when the hour had come and In a similar way with hands joined;

c) the words of the Lord, with each extending his right hand toward the bread and toward the chalice, if this seems appropriate; and at the elevation looking toward them and after this bowing profoundly;

d) the parts Therefore, O Lord, as we now celebrate and Look, O Lord, upon the Sacrifice with hands extended.

234. It is appropriate that the intercessions Therefore, Lord, remember now and To all of us, your children be assigned to one or other of the concelebrants, who pronounces them alone, with hands extended, and in a loud voice.

235. As for other Eucharistic Prayers approved by the Apostolic See, the norms laid down for each one are to be observed.

236. The concluding doxology of the Eucharistic Prayer is pronounced solely by the principal Priest Celebrant or together, if this is desired, with the other concelebrants, but not by the faithful.

The Communion Rite

237. Then the principal celebrant, with hands joined, says the introduction to the Lord's Prayer. Next, with hands extended, he says the Lord's Prayer itself together with the other concelebrants, who also pray with hands extended, and together with the people.

238. The Libera nos (*Deliver us*) is said by the principal celebrant alone, with hands extended. All the concelebrants, together with the people, pronounce the concluding acclamation For the kingdom.

239. After the Deacon or, in the absence of a Deacon, one of the concelebrants, has given the instruction Let us offer each

other the sign of peace, all give one another the Sign of Peace. Those concelebrants nearer the principal celebrant receive the Sign of Peace from him before the Deacon does.

240. During the Agnus Dei (*Lamb of God*), the Deacons or some of the concelebrants may help the principal celebrant to break the hosts for the Communion of both the concelebrants and the people.

241. After the commingling, the principal celebrant alone, with hands joined, quietly says either the prayer Domine Iesu Christe, Fili Dei vivi (*Lord Jesus Christ, Son of the living God*) or the prayer Perceptio Corporis et Sanguinis tui (*May the receiving of your Body and Blood*).

242. Once the prayer for Communion has been said, the principal celebrant genuflects and steps back a little. Then one after another the concelebrants come to the middle of the altar, genuflect, and reverently take the Body of Christ from the altar. Then holding it in their right hand, with the left hand placed underneath, they return to their places. However, the concelebrants may remain in their places and take the Body of Christ from the paten held for them by the principal celebrant or held by one or more of the concelebrants passing in front of them, or they may do so by handing the paten one to another, and so to the last of them.

243. Then the principal celebrant takes a host consecrated in the same Mass, holds it slightly raised above the paten or the chalice, and, facing the people, says the Ecce Agnus Dei (*Behold the Lamb of God*). With the concelebrants and the people he continues, saying the Domine, non sum dignus (*Lord, I am not worthy*).

244. Then the principal celebrant, facing the altar, says quietly, Corpus Christi custodiat me in vitam aeternam (*May the Body of Christ keep me safe for eternal life*), and reverently receives the Body of Christ. The concelebrants do likewise, giving themselves Communion. After them the Deacon receives the Body and Blood of the Lord from the principal celebrant.

245. The Blood of the Lord may be consumed either by drinking from the chalice directly, or by intinction, or by means of a tube or a spoon.

246. If Communion is consumed by drinking directly from the chalice, one of these procedures may be followed:

a) The principal celebrant, standing at the middle of the altar, takes the chalice and says quietly, Sanguis Christi custodiat me in vitam aeternam (*May the Blood of Christ keep me safe for eternal life*). He consumes a little of the Blood of Christ and hands the chalice to the Deacon or a concelebrant. He then distributes Communion to the faithful (*cf. nos. 160-162*).

The concelebrants approach the altar one after another or, if two chalices are used, two by two. They genuflect, partake of the Blood of Christ, wipe the rim of the chalice, and return to their seats.

b) The principal celebrant consumes the Blood of the Lord standing as usual at the middle of the altar.

The concelebrants, however, may partake of the Blood of the Lord while remaining in their places and drinking from the chalice presented to them by the Deacon or by one of the concelebrants, or even passed from one to the other. The chalice is always wiped either by the one who drinks from it or by the one who presents it. After each has communicated, he returns to his seat.

247. The Deacon reverently drinks at the altar all of the Blood of Christ that remains, assisted, if the case requires, by some of the concelebrants. He then carries the chalice to the credence table and there he or a duly instituted acolyte purifies it, wipes it, and arranges it as usual (*cf. no. 183*).

248. The Communion of the concelebrants may also be arranged in such a way that each communicates from the Body of the Lord at the altar and, immediately afterwards, from the Blood of the Lord.

In this case the principal celebrant receives Communion under both kinds in the usual way (*cf. no. 158*), observing, however, the rite chosen in each particular instance for Communion from the chalice; and the other concelebrants should do the same.

After the principal celebrant's Communion, the chalice is placed at the side of the altar on another corporal. The concelebrants approach the middle of the altar one by one, genuflect, and communicate from the Body of the Lord; then they move to the side of the altar and partake of the Blood of the Lord, following the rite chosen for Communion from the chalice, as has been remarked above.

The Communion of the Deacon and the purification of the chalice take place as described above.

249. If the concelebrants' Communion is by intinction, the principal celebrant partakes of the Body and Blood of the Lord in the usual way, but making sure that enough of the precious Blood remains in the chalice for the Communion of the concelebrants. Then the Deacon, or one of the concelebrants, arranges the chalice together with the paten containing particles of the host, if appropriate, either in the centre of the altar or at the side on another corporal.

The concelebrants approach the altar one by one, genuflect, and take a particle, intinct it partly into the chalice, and, holding a purificator under their mouth, consume the intincted particle. They then return to their places as at the beginning of Mass.

The Deacon also receives Communion by intinction and to the concelebrant's words, Corpus et Sanguis Christi (*The Body and Blood of Christ*) replies, Amen. Moreover, the Deacon consumes at the altar all that remains of the Precious Blood, assisted, if the case requires, by some of the concelebrants. He carries the chalice to the credence table and there he or a duly instituted acolyte purifies it, wipes it, and arranges it as usual.

The Concluding Rites

250. Everything else until the end of Mass is done by the principal celebrant in the usual way (*cf. nos. 166–168*), with the other concelebrants remaining at their seats.

251. Before leaving the altar, the concelebrants make a profound bow to the altar. For his part the principal celebrant, along with the Deacon, venerates the altar as usual with a kiss.

III. MASS AT WHICH ONLY ONE MINISTER PARTICIPATES

252. At a Mass celebrated by a Priest with only one minister to assist him and to make the responses, the rite of Mass with the people is followed (*cf. nos. 120-169*), the minister saying the people's parts if appropriate.

253. If, however, the minister is a Deacon, he performs his proper functions (*cf. nos. 171–186*) and likewise carries out the other parts, that is, those of the people.

254. Mass should not be celebrated without a minister, or at least one of the faithful, except for a just and reasonable cause. In this case, the greetings, the instructions, and the blessing at the end of Mass are omitted.

255. Before Mass, the necessary vessels are prepared either at the credence table or on the right hand side of the altar.

The Introductory Rites

256. The Priest approaches the altar and, after making a profound bow along with the minister, venerates the altar with a kiss and goes to the chair. If he wishes, the Priest may remain at the altar; in which case, the Missal is also prepared there. Then the minister or the Priest says the Entrance Antiphon.

257. Then the Priest, standing, makes with the minister the Sign of the Cross as the Priest says, In the name of the Father. Facing the minister, he greets him, choosing one of the formulas provided.

258. Then the Penitential Act takes place, and, in accordance with the rubrics, the Kyrie and the Gloria in excelsis (*Glory to God in the highest*) are said.

259. Then, with hands joined, the Priest pronounces, Let us pray, and after a suitable pause, with hands extended, he pronounces the Collect. At the end the minister acclaims, Amen.

The Liturgy of the Word

260. The readings should, insofar as possible, be proclaimed from the ambo or a lectern.

261. After the Collect, the minister reads the First Reading and Psalm, the Second Reading, when it is to be said, and the verse of the Alleluia or other chant.

262. Then the Priest, bowing profoundly, says the prayer Munda cor meum (*Cleanse my heart*) and after this reads the Gospel. At the end he says, The Gospel of the Lord, to which the minister replies, Praise to you, Lord Jesus Christ. The Priest then venerates the book with a kiss, saying quietly the formula Per evangelica dicta (*Through the words of the Gospel*).

263. After this, the Priest says the Symbol or Creed, in accordance with the rubrics, together with the minister.

264. The Universal Prayer follows, which may be said even in this form of Mass. The Priest introduces and concludes it, with the minister announcing the intentions.

The Liturgy of the Eucharist

265. In the Liturgy of the Eucharist, everything is done as at Mass with the people, except for the following.

266. After the acclamation at the end of the embolism that follows the Lord's Prayer, the Priest says the prayer Domine Iesu Christe, qui dixisti (*Lord Jesus Christ, who said to your Apostles*). He then adds, The peace of the Lord be with you always, to which the minister replies, And with your spirit. If appropriate, the Priest gives the Sign of Peace to the minister.

267. Then, while he says the Agnus Dei (*Lamb of God*) with the minister, the Priest breaks the host over the paten. After the Agnus Dei (*Lamb of God*), he performs the commingling, saying quietly the prayer Haec commixtio (*May this mingling*).

268. After the commingling, the Priest quietly says either the prayer Domine Iesu Christe, Fili Dei vivi (*Lord Jesus Christ, Son of the living God*) or the prayer Perceptio Corporis et Sanguinis tui (*May the receiving of your Body and Blood*). Then he genuflects, takes the host, and, if the minister is to receive Communion, turns to the minister and, holding the host a little above the paten or the chalice, says the Ecce Agnus Dei (*Behold the Lamb of God*), adding with the minister, Lord, I am not worthy. Then facing the altar, the Priest partakes of the Body of Christ. If, however, the minister does not receive Communion, the Priest, after genuflecting, takes the host and, facing the altar, says quietly, Lord, I am not worthy, etc., and the Corpus Christi custodiat me in vitam aeternam (*May the Body of Christ keep me safe for eternal life*), and consumes the Body of Christ. Then he takes the chalice and says quietly, Sanguis Christi custodiat me in vitam aeternam (*May the Blood of Christ keep me safe for eternal life*), and consumes the Blood of Christ.

269. Before Communion is given to the minister, the Communion Antiphon is said by the minister or by the Priest himself.

270. The Priest purifies the chalice at the credence table or at the altar. If the chalice is purified at the altar, it may be carried to the credence table by the minister or may be arranged once again on the altar, at the side.

271. After the purification of the chalice, the Priest should observe a brief pause for silence, and after this he says the Prayer after Communion.

The Concluding Rites

272. The Concluding Rites are carried out as at a Mass with the people, but the Ite, missa est (*Go forth, the Mass is ended*) is

omitted. The Priest venerates the altar as usual with a kiss and, after making a profound bow with the minister, withdraws.

IV. SOME GENERAL NORMS
FOR ALL FORMS OF MASS

Veneration of the Altar and the Book of the Gospels

273. According to traditional practice, the veneration of the altar and of the Book of the Gospels is done by means of a kiss. However, where a sign of this kind is not in harmony with the traditions or the culture of some region, it is for the Conference of Bishops to establish some other sign in its place, with the consent of the Apostolic See.

Genuflections and Bows

274. A genuflection, made by bending the right knee to the ground, signifies adoration, and therefore it is reserved for the Most Blessed Sacrament, as well as for the Holy Cross from the solemn adoration during the liturgical celebration on Good Friday until the beginning of the Easter Vigil.

During Mass, three genuflections are made by the Priest Celebrant: namely, after the elevation of the host, after the elevation of the chalice, and before Communion. Certain specific features to be observed in a concelebrated Mass are noted in their proper place (*cf. nos. 210–251*).

If, however, the tabernacle with the Most Blessed Sacrament is situated in the sanctuary, the Priest, the Deacon, and the other ministers genuflect when they approach the altar and when they depart from it, but not during the celebration of Mass itself.

Otherwise, all who pass before the Most Blessed Sacrament genuflect, unless they are moving in procession.

Ministers carrying the processional cross or candles bow their heads instead of genuflecting.

275. A bow signifies reverence and honour shown to the persons themselves or to the signs that represent them. There are two kinds of bow: a bow of the head and a bow of the body.

a) A bow of the head is made when the three Divine Persons are named together and at the names of Jesus, of the Blessed Virgin Mary, and of the Saint in whose honour Mass is being celebrated.

b) A bow of the body, that is to say, a profound bow, is made to the altar; during the prayers Munda cor meum (*Cleanse my heart*) and In spiritu humilitatis (*With humble spirit*); in the Creed at the words et incarnatus est (*and by the Holy Spirit...and became man*); in the Roman Canon at the Supplices te rogamus (*In humble prayer we ask you, almighty God*). The same kind of bow is made by the Deacon when he asks for a blessing before the proclamation of the Gospel. In addition, the Priest bows slightly as he pronounces the words of the Lord at the Consecration.

Incensation

276. Thurification or incensation is an expression of reverence and of prayer, as is signified in Sacred Scripture (cf. *Ps* 140 [141]: 2; *Rev* 8:3).

Incense may be used optionally in any form of Mass:

a) during the Entrance Procession;

b) at the beginning of Mass, to incense the cross and the altar;

c) at the procession before the Gospel and the proclamation of the Gospel itself;

d) after the bread and the chalice have been placed on the altar, to incense the offerings, the cross, and the altar, as well as the Priest and the people;

e) at the elevation of the host and the chalice after the Consecration.

277. The Priest, having put incense into the thurible, blesses it with the Sign of the Cross, without saying anything.

Before and after an incensation, a profound bow is made to the person or object that is incensed, except for the altar and the offerings for the Sacrifice of the Mass.

Three swings of the thurible are used to incense: the Most Blessed Sacrament, a relic of the Holy Cross and images of the Lord exposed for public veneration, the offerings for the Sacrifice of the Mass, the altar cross, the Book of the Gospels, the paschal candle, the Priest, and the people.

Two swings of the thurible are used to incense relics and images of the Saints exposed for public veneration; this should be done, however, only at the beginning of the celebration, following the incensation of the altar.

The altar is incensed with single swings of the thurible in this way:

a) if the altar is freestanding with respect to the wall, the Priest incenses walking around it;

b) if the altar is not freestanding, the Priest incenses it while walking first to the right hand side, then to the left.

The cross, if situated on the altar or near it, is incensed by the Priest before he incenses the altar; otherwise, he incenses it when he passes in front of it.

The Priest incenses the offerings with three swings of the thurible or by making the Sign of the Cross over the offerings with the thurible before going on to incense the cross and the altar.

The Purification

278. Whenever a fragment of the host adheres to his fingers, especially after the fraction or after the Communion of the faithful, the Priest should wipe his fingers over the paten or, if necessary, wash them. Likewise, he should also gather any fragments that may have fallen outside the paten.

279. The sacred vessels are purified by the Priest, the Deacon, or an instituted acolyte after Communion or after Mass, insofar as possible at the credence table. The purification of the chalice is done with water alone or with wine and water, which is then

consumed by whoever does the purification. The paten is wiped clean as usual with the purificator.

Care is to be taken that whatever may remain of the Blood of Christ after the distribution of Communion is consumed immediately and completely at the altar.

280. If a host or any particle should fall, it is to be picked up reverently; and if any of the Precious Blood is spilled, the area where the spill occurred should be washed with water, and this water should then be poured into the sacrarium in the sacristy.

Communion under Both Kinds

281. Holy Communion has a fuller form as a sign when it takes place under both kinds. For in this form the sign of the Eucharistic banquet is more clearly evident and clearer expression is given to the divine will by which the new and eternal Covenant is ratified in the Blood of the Lord, as also the connection between the Eucharistic banquet and the eschatological banquet in the Kingdom of the Father.[105]

282. Sacred pastors should take care to ensure that the faithful who participate in the rite or are present at it, are made aware by the most suitable means possible of the Catholic teaching on the form of Holy Communion as laid down by the Ecumenical Council of Trent. Above all, they should instruct the Christian faithful that the Catholic faith teaches that Christ, whole and entire, and the true Sacrament, is received even under only one species, and hence that as regards the resulting fruits, those who receive under only one species are not deprived of any grace that is necessary for salvation.[106]

Furthermore, they should teach that the Church, in her administration of the Sacraments, has the power to lay down or alter whatever provisions, apart from the substance of the Sacraments, that she judges to be more readily conducive to

---

[105] Cf. Sacred Congregation of Rites, Instruction, *Eucharisticum mysterium*, 25 May 1967, no. 32: *Acta Apostolicae Sedis* 59 (1967), p. 558.

[106] Cf. Ecumenical Council of Trent, Session XXI, *Doctrina de communione sub utraque specie et parvulorum*, 16 July 1562, cap. 1-3: Denzinger-Schönmetzer, nos. 1725-1729.

reverence for the Sacraments and the good of the recipients, in view of changing conditions, times, and places.[107] However, at the same time the faithful should be instructed to participate more readily in this sacred rite, by which the sign of the Eucharistic banquet is made more fully evident.

283. In addition to those cases given in the ritual books, Communion under both kinds is permitted for:

a) Priests who are not able to celebrate or concelebrate Mass;

b) the Deacon and others who perform some duty at the Mass;

c) members of communities at the Conventual Mass or the 'community' Mass, along with seminarians, and all those engaged in a retreat or taking part in a spiritual or pastoral gathering.

The Diocesan Bishop may establish norms for Communion under both kinds for his own diocese, which are also to be observed in churches of religious and at celebrations with small groups. The Diocesan Bishop is also given the faculty to permit Communion under both kinds whenever it may seem appropriate to the Priest to whom a community has been entrusted as its own shepherd, provided that the faithful have been well instructed and that there is no danger of profanation of the Sacrament or of the rite's becoming difficult because of the large number of participants or for some other cause.

As to the manner of distributing Holy Communion under both kinds to the faithful and the extent of the faculty for doing so, the Conferences of Bishops may publish norms, once their decisions have received the *recognitio* of the Apostolic See.

284. When Communion is distributed under both kinds:

a) the chalice is usually administered by a Deacon or, in the absence of a Deacon, by a Priest, or even by a duly instituted acolyte or another extraordinary minister of Holy Communion, or by one of the faithful who, in a case of necessity, has been entrusted with this duty for a single occasion;

---

[107] Cf. *ibidem,* cap. 2: Denzinger-Schönmetzer, no. 1728.

b) whatever may remain of the Blood of Christ is consumed at the altar by the Priest or the Deacon or the duly instituted acolyte who ministered the chalice. The same then purifies, wipes, and arranges the sacred vessels in the usual way.

Any of the faithful who wish to receive Holy Communion under the species of bread alone should be given Communion in this form.

285. For Communion under both kinds the following should be prepared:

a) If Communion from the chalice is done by drinking directly from the chalice, a chalice of a sufficiently large size or several chalices are prepared. However, care should be taken lest beyond what is needed of the Blood of Christ remains to be consumed at the end of the celebration.

b) If Communion from the chalice is done by intinction, the hosts should be neither too thin nor too small, but rather a little thicker than usual, so that after being intincted partly into the Blood of Christ they can still be easily distributed.

286. If Communion of the Blood of Christ is carried out by communicants' drinking from the chalice, each communicant, after receiving the Body of Christ, moves to the minister of the chalice and stands facing him. The minister says, The Blood of Christ, the communicant replies, Amen, and the minister hands over the chalice, which the communicant raises to his or her mouth. Each communicant drinks a little from the chalice, hands it back to the minister, and then withdraws; the minister wipes the rim of the chalice with the purificator.

287. If Communion from the chalice is carried out by intinction, each communicant, holding a Communion-plate under the mouth, approaches the Priest who holds a vessel with the sacred particles, with a minister standing at his side and holding the chalice. The Priest takes a host, intincts it partly in the chalice and, showing it, says, The Body and Blood of Christ. The communicant replies, Amen, receives the Sacrament in the mouth from the Priest, and then withdraws.

CHAPTER V

THE ARRANGEMENT AND ORNAMENTATION
OF CHURCHES
FOR THE CELEBRATION OF THE EUCHARIST

I. GENERAL PRINCIPLES

288. For the celebration of the Eucharist, the People of God are normally gathered together in a church or, if there is no church or if it is too small, then in another respectable place that is nonetheless worthy of so great a mystery. Therefore, churches or other places should be suitable for carrying out the sacred action and for ensuring the active participation of the faithful. Moreover, sacred buildings and requisites for divine worship should be truly worthy and beautiful and be signs and symbols of heavenly realities.[108]

289. Consequently, the Church constantly seeks the noble assistance of the arts and admits the artistic expressions of all peoples and regions.[109] In fact, just as she is intent on preserving the works of art and the artistic treasures handed down from past centuries[110] and, insofar as necessary, on adapting them to new needs, so also she strives to promote new works of art that are in harmony with the character of each successive age.[111]

---

[108] Cf. Second Ecumenical Council of the Vatican, Constitution on the Sacred Liturgy, *Sacrosanctum Concilium*, nos. 122-124; Decree on the Ministry and Life of Priests, *Presbyterorum ordinis*, no. 5; Sacred Congregation of Rites, Instruction, *Inter Oecumenici*, 26 September 1964, no. 90: *Acta Apostolicae Sedis* 56 (1964), p. 897; Instruction, *Eucharisticum mysterium*, 25 May 1967, no. 24: *Acta Apostolicae Sedis* 59 (1967), p. 554; Code of Canon Law, *Codex Iuris Canonici*, can. 932 § 1

[109] Cf. Second Ecumenical Council of the Vatican, Constitution on the Sacred Liturgy, *Sacrosanctum Concilium*, no. 123.

[110] Cf. Sacred Congregation of Rites, Instruction, *Eucharisticum mysterium*, 25 May 1967, no. 24: *Acta Apostolicae Sedis* 59 (1967), p. 554.

[111] Cf. Second Ecumenical Council of the Vatican, Constitution on the Sacred Liturgy, *Sacrosanctum Concilium*, nos. 123, 129; Sacred Congregation of Rites, Instruction, *Inter Oecumenici*, 26 September 1964, no. 13c: *Acta Apostolicae Sedis* 56 (1964), p. 880.

On account of this, in appointing artists and choosing works of art to be admitted into a church, what should be looked for is that true excellence in art which nourishes faith and devotion and accords authentically with both the meaning and the purpose for which it is intended.[112]

290.   All churches should be dedicated or at least blessed. Cathedrals and parish churches, however, are to be dedicated with a solemn rite.

291.   For the proper construction, restoration, and arrangement of sacred buildings, all those involved should consult the diocesan commission for the Sacred Liturgy and sacred art. Moreover, the Diocesan Bishop should employ the counsel and help of this commission whenever it comes to laying down norms on this matter, approving plans for new buildings, and making decisions on the more important matters.[113]

292.   The ornamentation of a church should contribute toward its noble simplicity rather than to ostentation. Moreover, in the choice of elements attention should be paid to authenticity and there should be the intention of fostering the instruction of the faithful and the dignity of the entire sacred place.

293.   The suitable arrangement of a church, and of what goes with it, in such a way as to meet appropriately the needs of our own age requires not only that care be taken as regards whatever pertains more immediately to the celebration of sacred actions but also that the faithful be provided with whatever is conducive to their appropriate comfort and is normally provided in places where people habitually gather.

294.   The People of God which is gathered for Mass is coherently and hierarchically ordered, and this finds its expression in the variety of ministries and the variety of actions according to the different parts of the celebration. Hence the general

---

[112] Cf. Second Ecumenical Council of the Vatican, Constitution on the Sacred Liturgy, *Sacrosanctum Concilium*, no. 123.

[113] Cf. *ibidem*, no. 126; Sacred Congregation of Rites, Instruction, *Inter Oecumenici*, 26 September 1964, no. 91: *Acta Apostolicae Sedis* 56 (1964), p. 898.

arrangement of the sacred building must be such that in some way it conveys the image of the assembled congregation and allows the appropriate ordering of all the participants, as well as facilitating each in the proper carrying out of his function.

The faithful and the *schola cantorum* (choir) shall have a place that facilitates their active participation.[114]

The Priest Celebrant, the Deacon, and the other ministers have places in the sanctuary. There, also, should be prepared seats for concelebrants, but if their number is great, seats should be arranged in another part of the church, though near the altar.

All these elements, even though they must express the hierarchical structure and the diversity of functions, should nevertheless bring about a close and coherent unity that is clearly expressive of the unity of the entire holy people. Indeed, the nature and beauty of the place and all its furnishings should foster devotion and express visually the holiness of the mysteries celebrated there.

II. ARRANGEMENT OF THE SANCTUARY FOR THE SACRED SYNAXIS

295. The sanctuary is the place where the altar stands, the Word of God is proclaimed, and the Priest, the Deacon, and the other ministers exercise their functions. It should be appropriately marked off from the body of the church either by its being somewhat elevated or by a particular structure and ornamentation. It should, moreover, be large enough to allow the Eucharist to be easily celebrated and seen.[115]

The Altar and its Ornamentation

296. The altar, on which is effected the Sacrifice of the Cross made present under sacramental signs, is also the table of the Lord to which the People of God is convoked to participate in

---

[114] Cf. Sacred Congregation of Rites, Instruction, *Inter Oecumenici*, 26 September 1964, nos. 97-98: *Acta Apostolicae Sedis* 56 (1964), p. 899.

[115] Cf. *ibidem*, no. 91: p. 898.

the Mass, and it is also the centre of the thanksgiving that is accomplished through the Eucharist.

297. The celebration of the Eucharist in a sacred place is to take place on an altar; however, outside a sacred place, it may take place on a suitable table, always with the use of a cloth, a corporal, a cross, and candles.

298. It is desirable that in every church there be a fixed altar, since this more clearly and permanently signifies Christ Jesus, the Living Stone (1 *Pt* 2:4; cf. *Eph* 2:20). In other places set aside for sacred celebrations, the altar may be movable.

An altar is said to be fixed if it is so constructed as to be attached to the floor and not removable; it is said to be movable if it can be displaced.

299. The altar should be built separate from the wall, in such a way that it is possible to walk around it easily and that Mass can be celebrated at it facing the people, which is desirable wherever possible. Moreover, the altar should occupy a place where it is truly the centre toward which the attention of the whole congregation of the faithful naturally turns.[116] The altar should usually be fixed and dedicated.

300. An altar, whether fixed or movable, should be dedicated according to the rite prescribed in the Roman Pontifical; but it is permissible for a movable altar simply to be blessed.

301. In keeping with the Church's traditional practice and with what the altar signifies, the table of a fixed altar should be of stone and indeed of natural stone.

However, other dignified, solid and well-crafted material may also be used according to the judgement of the Conference of Bishops. As to the supports or base for supporting the table, these may be made of any material, provided it is dignified and solid.

A movable altar may be constructed of any noble and solid material suited to liturgical use, according to the traditions and usages of the different regions.

---

[116] Cf. *ibidem.*

In England and Wales, and in Scotland: In keeping with the Church's traditional practice and with what the altar signifies, the table of a fixed altar should be of stone and indeed of natural stone or, in the dioceses of England and Wales, and of Scotland, it may be made of wood which is dignified, solid and well-crafted, provided that the altar is structurally immobile. As to the supports or base for supporting the table, these may be made of any material, provided it is dignified and solid.

A movable altar may be constructed of any noble and solid material suited to liturgical use, according to the traditions and usages of the different regions.

302. The practice of the deposition of relics of Saints, even those not Martyrs, under the altar to be dedicated is fittingly retained. However, care should be taken to ensure the authenticity of such relics.

303. In building new churches, it is preferable for a single altar to be erected, one that in the gathering of the faithful will signify the one Christ and the one Eucharist of the Church.

In already existing churches, however, when the old altar is so positioned that it makes the people's participation difficult but cannot be moved without damage to artistic value, another fixed altar, skilfully made and properly dedicated, should be erected and the sacred rites celebrated on it alone. In order that the attention of the faithful not be distracted from the new altar, the old altar should not be decorated in any special way.

304. Out of reverence for the celebration of the memorial of the Lord and for the banquet in which the Body and Blood of the Lord are offered, there should be, on an altar where this is celebrated, at least one cloth, white in colour, whose shape, size, and decoration are in keeping with the altar's structure.

305. Moderation should be observed in the decoration of the altar.

During Advent the floral decoration of the altar should be marked by a moderation suited to the character of this time of year, without expressing in anticipation the full joy of the Nativity of the Lord. During Lent it is forbidden for the altar to be decorated with flowers. Exceptions, however, are Laetare Sunday (Fourth Sunday of Lent), Solemnities, and Feasts.

Floral decoration should always show moderation and be arranged around the altar rather than on the altar table.

306. For only what is required for the celebration of the Mass may be placed on the altar table: namely, from the beginning of the celebration until the proclamation of the Gospel, the Book of the Gospels; then from the Presentation of the Gifts until the purification of the vessels, the chalice with the paten, a ciborium, if necessary, and, finally, the corporal, the purificator, the pall, and the Missal.

In addition, arranged discreetly, there should be whatever may be needed to amplify the Priest's voice.

307. The candlesticks required for the different liturgical services for reasons of reverence or the festive character of the celebration (*cf. no. 117*), should be appropriately placed either on the altar or around it, according to the design of the altar and the sanctuary, so that the whole may be harmonious and the faithful may not be impeded from a clear view of what takes place at the altar or what is placed upon it.

308. Likewise, either on the altar or near it, there is to be a cross, with the figure of Christ crucified upon it, a cross clearly visible to the assembled people. It is desirable that such a cross should remain near the altar even outside of liturgical celebrations, so as to call to mind for the faithful the saving Passion of the Lord.

The Ambo

309. The dignity of the Word of God requires that in the church there be a suitable place from which it may be proclaimed and toward which the attention of the faithful naturally turns during the Liturgy of the Word.[117]

---

[117] Cf. Sacred Congregation of Rites, Instruction, *Inter Oecumenici*, 26 September 1964, no. 92: *Acta Apostolicae Sedis* 56 (1964), p. 899.

It is appropriate that generally this place be a stationary ambo and not simply a movable lectern. The ambo must be located in keeping with the design of each church in such a way that the ordained ministers and readers may be clearly seen and heard by the faithful.

From the ambo only the readings, the Responsorial Psalm, and the Easter Proclamation (*Exsultet*) are to be proclaimed; likewise it may be used for giving the Homily and for announcing the intentions of the Universal Prayer. The dignity of the ambo requires that only a minister of the word should stand at it.

It is appropriate that before being put into liturgical use a new ambo be blessed according to the rite described in the Roman Ritual.[118]

The Chair for the Priest Celebrant and Other Seats

310. The chair of the Priest Celebrant must signify his function of presiding over the gathering and of directing the prayer. Thus the more suitable place for the chair is facing the people at the head of the sanctuary, unless the design of the building or other features prevent this: as, for example, if on account of too great a distance, communication between the Priest and the congregation would be difficult, or if the tabernacle were to be positioned in the centre behind the altar. In any case, any appearance of a throne is to be avoided.[119] It is appropriate that before being put into liturgical use, the chair be blessed according to the rite described in the Roman Ritual.[120]

Likewise, seats should be arranged in the sanctuary for concelebrating Priests as well as for Priests who are present at the celebration in choir dress but without concelebrating.

The seat for the Deacon should be placed near that of the celebrant. For the other ministers seats should be arranged so

---

[118] Cf. Rituale Romanum, *De Benedictionibus*, editio typica, 1984, Ordo benedictionis occasione data auspicandi novum ambonem, nos. 900-918.

[119] Cf. Sacred Congregation of Rites, Instruction, *Inter Oecumenici*, 26 September 1964, no. 92: *Acta Apostolicae Sedis* 56 (1964), p. 898.

[120] Cf. Rituale Romanum, *De Benedictionibus*, editio typica, 1984, Ordo benedictionis occasione data auspicandi novam cathedram seu sedem praesidentiae, nos. 880-899.

that they are clearly distinguishable from seats for the clergy and so that the ministers are easily able to carry out the function entrusted to them.[121]

III. THE ARRANGEMENT OF THE CHURCH

The Places for the Faithful

311. Places for the faithful should be arranged with appropriate care so that they are able to participate in the sacred celebrations, duly following them with their eyes and their attention. It is desirable that benches or seating usually should be provided for their use. However, the custom of reserving seats for private persons is to be reprobated.[122] Moreover, benches or seating should be so arranged, especially in newly built churches, that the faithful can easily take up the bodily postures required for the different parts of the celebration and can have easy access for the reception of Holy Communion

Care should be taken to ensure that the faithful be able not only to see the Priest, the Deacon, and the readers but also, with the aid of modern technical means, to hear them without difficulty.

The Place for the Schola Cantorum and the Musical Instruments

312. The *schola cantorum* (choir) should be so positioned with respect to the arrangement of each church that its nature may be clearly evident, namely as part of the assembled community of the faithful undertaking a specific function. The positioning should also help the choir to exercise this function more easily and allow each choir member full sacramental participation in the Mass in a convenient manner.[123]

---

[121] Cf. Sacred Congregation of Rites, Instruction, *Inter Oecumenici*, 26 September 1964, no. 92: *Acta Apostolicae Sedis* 56 (1964), p. 898.

[122] Cf. Second Ecumenical Council of the Vatican, Constitution on the Sacred Liturgy, *Sacrosanctum Concilium*, no. 32.

[123] Cf. Sacred Congregation of Rites, Instruction, *Musicam sacram*, 5 March 1967, no. 23: *Acta Apostolicae Sedis* 59 (1967), p. 307.

313. The organ and other lawfully approved musical instruments should be placed in a suitable place so that they can sustain the singing of both the choir and the people and be heard with ease by everybody if they are played alone. It is appropriate that before being put into liturgical use, the organ be blessed according to the rite described in the Roman Ritual.[124]

In Advent the use of the organ and other musical instruments should be marked by a moderation suited to the character of this time of year, without expressing in anticipation the full joy of the Nativity of the Lord.

In Lent the playing of the organ and musical instruments is allowed only in order to support the singing. Exceptions, however, are Laetare Sunday (Fourth Sunday of Lent), Solemnities, and Feasts.

The Place for the Reservation of the Most Holy Eucharist

314. In accordance with the structure of each church and legitimate local customs, the Most Blessed Sacrament should be reserved in a tabernacle in a part of the church that is truly noble, prominent, conspicuous, worthily decorated, and suitable for prayer.[125]

The tabernacle should usually be the only one, be irremovable, be made of solid and inviolable material that is not transparent, and be locked in such a way that the danger of profanation is prevented to the greatest extent possible.[126] Moreover, it is appropriate that before it is put into liturgical

---

[124] Cf. Rituale Romanum, *De Benedictionibus*, editio typica, 1984, Ordo benedictionis organi, nos. 1052-1067.

[125] Cf. Sacred Congregation of Rites, Instruction, *Eucharisticum mysterium*, 25 May 1967, no. 54: *Acta Apostolicae Sedis* 59 (1967), p. 568; cf. also Instruction, *Inter Oecumenici*, 26 September 1964, no. 95: *Acta Apostolicae Sedis* 56 (1964), p. 898.

[126] Cf. Sacred Congregation of Rites, Instruction, *Eucharisticum mysterium*, 25 May 1967, no. 52: *Acta Apostolicae Sedis* 59 (1967), p. 568; Sacred Congregation of Rites, Instruction, *Inter Oecumenici*, 26 September 1964, no. 95: *Acta Apostolicae Sedis* 56 (1964), p. 898; Sacred Congregation for the Sacraments, Instruction, *Nullo umquam tempore*, 28 May 1938, no. 4: *Acta Apostolicae Sedis* 30 (1938), pp. 199-200; Rituale Romanum, *De sacra Communione et de cultu mysterii eucharistici extra Missam*, editio typica, 1973, nos. 10-11; Code of Canon Law, *Codex Iuris Canonici*, can. 938 § 3.

use, the tabernacle be blessed according to the rite described in the Roman Ritual.[127]

315. It is more appropriate as a sign that on an altar on which Mass is celebrated there not be a tabernacle in which the Most Holy Eucharist is reserved.[128]

Consequently, it is preferable that the tabernacle be located, according to the judgement of the Diocesan Bishop:

a) either in the sanctuary, apart from the altar of celebration, in a appropriate form and place, not excluding its being positioned on an old altar no longer used for celebration (*cf. no. 303*);

b) or even in some chapel suitable for the private adoration and prayer of the faithful[129] and organically connected to the church and readily noticeable by the Christian faithful.

316. In accordance with traditional custom, near the tabernacle a special lamp, fuelled by oil or wax, should shine permanently to indicate the presence of Christ and honour it.[130]

317. In no way should any of the other things be forgotten which are prescribed by law concerning the reservation of the Most Holy Eucharist.[131]

---

[127] Cf. Rituale Romanum, *De Benedictionibus*, editio typica, 1984, Ordo benedictionis occasione data auspicandi novum tabernaculum eucharisticum, nos. 919-929.

[128] Cf. Sacred Congregation of Rites, Instruction, *Eucharisticum mysterium*, 25 May 1967, no. 55: *Acta Apostolicae Sedis* 59 (1967), p. 569.

[129] *Ibidem*, no. 53: *Acta Apostolicae Sedis* 59 (1967), p. 568; Rituale Romanum, *De sacra Communione et de cultu mysterii eucharistici extra Missam*, editio typica, 1973, no. 9; Code of Canon Law, *Codex Iuris Canonici*, can. 938 §2; John Paul II, Apostolic Letter, *Dominicae Cenae*, 24 February 1980, no. 3: *Acta Apostolicae Sedis* (1980), pp. 117-119.

[130] Cf. Code of Canon Law, *Codex Iuris Canonici*, can. 940; Sacred Congregation of Rites, Instruction, *Eucharisticum mysterium*, 25 May 1967, no. 57: *Acta Apostolicae Sedis* 59 (1967), p. 569; cf. Rituale Romanum, *De sacra Communione et de cultu mysterii eucharistici extra Missam*, editio typica, 1973, no. 11.

[131] Cf. particularly in Sacred Congregation for the Sacraments, Instruction, *Nullo umquam tempore*, 28 May 1938: *Acta Apostolicae Sedis* 30 (1938), pp. 198-207; Code of Canon Law, *Codex Iuris Canonici*, cann. 934-944.

Sacred Images

318. In the earthly Liturgy, the Church participates, by a foretaste, in that heavenly Liturgy which is celebrated in the holy city of Jerusalem, toward which she journeys as a pilgrim, and where Christ is seated at the right hand of God; and by venerating the memory of the Saints, she hopes one day to have some share and fellowship with them.[132]

Thus, in sacred buildings images of the Lord, of the Blessed Virgin Mary, and of the Saints, in accordance with most ancient tradition of the Church, should be displayed for veneration by the faithful[133] and should be so arranged so as to lead the faithful toward the mysteries of faith celebrated there. Care should, therefore, be taken that their number not be increased indiscriminately, and moreover that they be arranged in proper order so as not to draw the attention of the faithful to themselves and away from the celebration itself.[134] There should usually be only one image of any given Saint. Generally speaking, in the ornamentation and arrangement of a church, as far as images are concerned, provision should be made for the devotion of the entire community as well as for the beauty and dignity of the images.

---

[132] Cf. Second Ecumenical Council of the Vatican, Constitution on the Liturgy, *Sacrosanctum Concilium*, no. 8.

[133] Cf. Pontificale Romanum, *Ordo Dedicationis ecclesiae et altaris*, editio typica, 1977, cap. IV, no. 10; Rituale Romanum, *De Benedictionibus*, editio typica, 1984, Ordo ad benedicendas imagines quae fidelium venerationi publicae exhibentur, nos. 984-1031.

[134] Cf. Second Ecumenical Council of the Vatican, Constitution on the Sacred Liturgy, *Sacrosanctum Concilium*, no. 125.

CHAPTER VI

THE REQUISITES FOR THE CELEBRATION OF MASS

I. THE BREAD AND WINE FOR CELEBRATING THE EUCHARIST

319. Following the example of Christ, the Church has always used bread and wine with water to celebrate the Lord's Supper.

320. The bread for celebrating the Eucharist must be made only from wheat, must be recently made, and, according to the ancient tradition of the Latin Church, must be unleavened.

321. By reason of the sign, it is required that the material for the Eucharistic Celebration truly have the appearance of food. Therefore, it is desirable that the Eucharistic Bread, even though unleavened and made in the traditional form, be fashioned in such a way that the Priest at Mass with the people is truly able to break it into parts and distribute these to at least some of the faithful. However, small hosts are not at all excluded when the large number of those receiving Holy Communion or other pastoral reasons call for them. Moreover, the gesture of the fraction or breaking of bread, which was quite simply the term by which the Eucharist was known in apostolic times, will bring out more clearly the force and importance of the sign of the unity of all in the one bread, and of the sign of charity by the fact that the one bread is distributed among the brothers and sisters.

322. The wine for the celebration of the Eucharist must be from the fruit of the vine (cf. *Lk* 22:18), natural, and unadulterated, that is, without admixture of extraneous substances.

323. Diligent care should be taken to ensure that the bread and wine intended for the Eucharist are kept in a perfect state of conservation: that is, that the wine does not turn to vinegar nor the bread spoil or become too hard to be broken easily.

324. If after the Consecration or as he receives Communion, the Priest notices that not wine but only water was poured into the chalice, he pours the water into some container, pours wine with water into the chalice and consecrates it, saying the part of narrative relating to the Consecration of the chalice, without being obliged to consecrate the bread again.

II. SACRED FURNISHINGS IN GENERAL

325. As in the case of the building of churches, so also regarding all sacred furnishings, the Church admits the manner of art of each individual region and accepts those adaptations that are in keeping with the culture and traditions of the individual nations, provided that all are suited to the purpose for which the sacred furnishings are intended.[135]

In this matter as well, that noble simplicity should be ensured which is the best accompaniment of genuine art.

326. In choosing materials for sacred furnishings, besides those which are traditional, others are admissible that, according to the mentality of our own age, are considered to be noble and are durable, and well suited for sacred use. Of these matters the Conference of Bishops in each region will be the judge (*cf. no. 390*).

III. SACRED VESSELS

327. Among the requisites for the celebration of Mass, the sacred vessels are held in special honour, and among these especially the chalice and paten, in which the bread and wine are offered and consecrated and from which they are consumed.

328. Sacred vessels should be made from precious metal. If they are made from metal that rusts or from a metal less precious than gold, they should generally be gilded on the inside.

---

[135] Cf. Second Ecumenical Council of the Vatican, Constitution on the Sacred Liturgy, *Sacrosanctum Concilium*, no. 128.

329. According to the judgement of the Conference of Bishops, its decisions having received the *recognitio* of the Apostolic See, sacred vessels may also be made from other solid materials which in the common estimation in each region are considered precious or noble, for example, ebony or other harder woods, provided that such materials are suitable for sacred use. In this case, preference is always to be given to materials that do not easily break or deteriorate. This applies to all vessels that are intended to hold the hosts, such as the paten, the ciborium, the pyx, the monstrance, and others of this kind.

330. As regards chalices and other vessels that are intended to serve as receptacles for the Blood of the Lord, they are to have a bowl of material that does not absorb liquids. The base, on the other hand, may be made of other solid and worthy materials.

331. For the Consecration of hosts, a large paten may fittingly be used, on which is placed the bread both for the Priest and the Deacon and also for the other ministers and for the faithful.

332. As regards the form of the sacred vessels, it is for the artist to fashion them in a manner that is more particularly in keeping with the customs of each region, provided the individual vessels are suitable for their intended liturgical use and are clearly distinguishable from vessels intended for everyday use.

333. As for the blessing of sacred vessels, the rites prescribed in the liturgical books should be followed.[136]

334. The practice should be kept of building in the sacristy a sacrarium into which is poured the water from the washing of sacred vessels and linens (*cf. no. 280*).

---

[136] Cf. Pontificale Romanum, *Ordo Dedicationis ecclesiae et altaris*, editio typica, 1977, Ordo benedictionis calicis et patenae; Rituale Romanum, *De Benedictionibus*, editio typica, 1984, Ordo benedictionis rerum quae in liturgicis celebrationibus usurpantur, nos. 1068-1084.

IV. SACRED VESTMENTS

335. In the Church, which is the Body of Christ, not all members have the same function. This diversity of offices is shown outwardly in the celebration of the Eucharist by the diversity of sacred vestments, which must therefore be a sign of the function proper to each minister. Moreover, these same sacred vestments should also contribute to the decoration of the sacred action itself. The vestments worn by Priests and Deacons, as well as the attire worn by lay ministers, are blessed before being put into liturgical use according to the rite described in the Roman Ritual.[137]

336. The sacred garment common to all ordained and instituted ministers of any rank is the alb, to be tied at the waist with a cincture unless it is made so as to fit even without such. Before the alb is put on, should this not completely cover the ordinary clothing at the neck, an amice should be used. The alb may not be exchanged for a surplice, not even over a cassock, on occasions when a chasuble or dalmatic is to be worn or when, according to the norms, only a stole is worn without a chasuble or dalmatic.

337. The vestment proper to the Priest Celebrant at Mass and during other sacred actions directly connected with Mass is the chasuble worn, unless otherwise indicated, over the alb and stole.

338. The vestment proper to the Deacon is the dalmatic, worn over the alb and stole; however, the dalmatic may be omitted out of necessity or on account of a lesser degree of solemnity.

339. Acolytes, readers, and other lay ministers may wear the alb or other suitable attire that has been legitimately approved by the Conference of Bishops (*cf. no. 390*).

---

[137] Cf. Rituale Romanum, *De Benedictionibus*, editio typica, 1984, Ordo benedictionis rerum quae in liturgicis celebrationibus usurpantur, no. 1070.

340. The stole is worn by the Priest around his neck and hanging down in front of his chest, while it is worn by the Deacon over his left shoulder and drawn diagonally across the chest to the right side, where it is fastened.

341. The cope is worn by the Priest in processions and during other sacred actions, in accordance with the rubrics proper to the individual rites.

342. As regards the form of sacred vestments, Conferences of Bishops may determine and propose to the Apostolic See adaptations that correspond to the needs and the usages of the individual regions.[138]

343. For making sacred vestments, in addition to traditional materials, natural fabrics proper to each region may be used, and also artificial fabrics that are in keeping with the dignity of the sacred action and the sacred person. The Conference of Bishops will be the judge of this matter.[139]

344. It is fitting that the beauty and nobility of each vestment not be sought in an abundance of overlaid ornamentation, but rather in the material used and in the design. Ornamentation on vestments should, moreover, consist of figures, that is, of images or symbols, that denote sacred use, avoiding anything unbecoming to this.

345. Diversity of colour in the sacred vestments has as its purpose to give more effective expression even outwardly whether to the specific character of the mysteries of faith to be celebrated or to a sense of Christian life's passage through the course of the liturgical year.

346. As regards the colour of sacred vestments, traditional usage should be observed, namely:

---

[138] Cf. Second Ecumenical Council of the Vatican, Constitution on the Sacred Liturgy, *Sacrosanctum Concilium*, no. 128.

[139] Cf. *ibidem*.

a) The colour white is used in the Offices and Masses during Easter Time and Christmas Time; and furthermore on celebrations of the Lord other than of his Passion, celebrations of the Blessed Virgin Mary, of the Holy Angels, and of Saints who were not Martyrs; on the Solemnities of All Saints (1 November) and of the Nativity of St. John the Baptist (24 June); and on the Feasts of St. John the Evangelist (27 December), of the Chair of St. Peter (22 February), and of the Conversion of St. Paul (25 January).

In England and Wales, and in Scotland: a) The colour white is used in the Offices and Masses during Easter Time and Christmas Time; on the Solemnity of the Most Holy Trinity, and furthermore on celebrations of the Lord other than of his Passion, celebrations of the Blessed Virgin Mary, of the Holy Angels, and of Saints who were not Martyrs; on the Solemnities of All Saints (1 November) and of the Nativity of St. John the Baptist (24 June); and on the Feasts of St. John the Evangelist (27 December), of the Chair of St. Peter (22 February), and of the Conversion of St. Paul (25 January). The colour white may also be worn by way of exception in Offices and Masses for the dead in the dioceses of England and Wales, and of Scotland.

---

b) The colour red is used on Palm Sunday of the Lord's Passion and on Friday of Holy Week, on Pentecost Sunday, on celebrations of the Lord's Passion, on the 'birthday' feast days of Apostles and Evangelists, and on celebrations of Martyr Saints.

c) The colour green is used in the Offices and Masses of Ordinary Time.

d) The colour violet or purple is used in Advent and Lent. It may also be worn in Offices and Masses for the Dead.

e) The colour black may be used, where it is the practice, in Masses for the Dead.

f) The colour rose may be used, where it is the practice, on Gaudete Sunday (Third Sunday of Advent) and on Laetare Sunday (Fourth Sunday of Lent).

g) On more solemn days, festive, that is, more precious, sacred vestments may be used even if not of the colour of the day.

Moreover, Conferences of Bishops may determine and propose to the Apostolic See adaptations regarding liturgical colours that correspond to the needs and culture of peoples.

347. Ritual Masses are celebrated in their proper colour, in white, or in a festive colour; Masses for Various Needs, on the other hand, are celebrated in the colour proper to the day or the time of year or in violet if they have a penitential character, for example, nos. 31, 33 or 38; Votive Masses are celebrated in the colour suited to the Mass itself or even in the colour proper to the day or the time of the year.

V. OTHER THINGS INTENDED FOR CHURCH USE

348. Besides the sacred vessels and the sacred vestments, for which some particular material is prescribed, other furnishings that either are intended for direct liturgical use[140] or are in any other way admitted into a church should be worthy and in keeping with their particular intended purpose.

349. Special care must be taken to ensure that the liturgical books, particularly the Book of the Gospels and the Lectionary, which are intended for the proclamation of the Word of God and hence receive special veneration, are to be in a liturgical action truly signs and symbols of higher realities and hence should be truly worthy, dignified, and beautiful.

350. Furthermore, every care is to be taken with respect to those things directly associated with the altar and the

---

[140] For blessing objects that are intended for liturgical use in churches, cf. Rituale Romanum, *De Benedictionibus*, editio typica, 1984, pars III.

celebration of the Eucharist, for example, the altar cross and the cross carried in procession.

351. Every effort should be made, even in minor matters, to observe appropriately the requirements of art and to ensure that a noble simplicity is combined with elegance.

CHAPTER VII

THE CHOICE OF THE MASS AND ITS PARTS

352. The pastoral effectiveness of a celebration will be greatly increased if the texts of the readings, the prayers and the liturgical chants correspond as aptly as possible to the needs, the preparation and the culture of the participants. This will be achieved by appropriate use of the many possibilities of choice described below.

Hence in arranging the celebration of Mass, the Priest should be attentive rather to the common spiritual good of the People of God than to his own inclinations. He should also remember that choices of this kind are to be made in harmony with those who exercise some part in the celebration, including the faithful, as regards the parts that more directly pertain to them.

Since, indeed, many possibilities are provided for choosing the different parts of the Mass, it is necessary for the Deacon, the readers, the psalmist, the cantor, the commentator, and the choir to know properly before the celebration the texts that concern each and that are to be used and it is necessary that nothing be in any sense improvised. For harmonious ordering and carrying out of the rites will greatly help in disposing the faithful for participation in the Eucharist.

I. THE CHOICE OF MASS

353. On Solemnities the Priest is obliged to follow the Calendar of the church where he is celebrating.

354. On Sundays, on the weekdays during Advent, Christmas Time, Lent, and Easter Time, on Feasts, and on Obligatory Memorials:

a) If Mass is celebrated with the people, the Priest should follow the Calendar of the church where he is celebrating;

b) If Mass is celebrated with the participation of one minister only, the Priest may choose either the Calendar of the church or his proper Calendar.

355. On Optional Memorials,

a) On the weekdays of Advent from 17 December to 24 December, on days within the Octave of the Nativity of the Lord, and on the weekdays of Lent, except Ash Wednesday and during Holy Week, the Mass texts for the current liturgical day are used; but the Collect may be taken from a Memorial which happens to be inscribed in the General Calendar for that day, except on Ash Wednesday and during Holy Week. On weekdays of Easter Time, Memorials of Saints may rightly be celebrated in full.

b) On weekdays of Advent before 17 December, on weekdays of Christmas Time from 2 January, and on weekdays of Easter Time, one of the following may be chosen: either the Mass of the weekday, or the Mass of the Saint or of one of the Saints whose Memorial is observed, or the Mass of any Saint inscribed in the Martyrology for that day.

c) On weekdays in Ordinary Time, there may be chosen either the Mass of the weekday, or the Mass of an Optional Memorial which happens to occur on that day, or the Mass of any Saint inscribed in the Martyrology for that day, or a Mass for Various Needs, or a Votive Mass.

If he celebrates with the people, the Priest will take care not to omit too frequently and without sufficient reason the readings assigned each day in the Lectionary to the weekdays, for the Church desires that a richer portion at the table of God's Word should be spread before the people.[141]

For the same reason he should choose Masses for the Dead in moderation, for every Mass is offered for both the living and the dead, and there is a commemoration of the dead in the Eucharistic Prayer.

---

[141] Cf. Second Ecumenical Council of the Vatican, Constitution on the Sacred Liturgy, *Sacrosanctum Concilium*, no. 51.

Where, however, the Optional Memorials of the Blessed Virgin Mary or of the Saints are dear to the faithful, the legitimate devotion of the latter should be satisfied.

Moreover, as regards the option of choosing between a Memorial inscribed in the General Calendar and one inserted in a diocesan or religious Calendar, preference should be given, all else being equal and in keeping with tradition, to the Memorial in the particular Calendar.

II. THE CHOICE OF TEXTS FOR THE MASS

356. In choosing texts for the different parts of the Mass, whether for the time of the year or for Saints, the norms that follow should be observed.

The Readings

357. Sundays and Solemnities have assigned to them three readings, that is, from a Prophet, an Apostle, and a Gospel, by which the Christian people are instructed in the continuity of the work of salvation according to God's wonderful design. These readings should be followed strictly. In Easter Time, according to the tradition of the Church, instead of being from the Old Testament, the reading is taken from the Acts of the Apostles.

For Feasts, two readings are assigned. If, however, according to the norms a Feast is raised to the rank of a Solemnity, a third reading is added, and this is taken from the Common.

For Memorials of Saints, unless proper readings are given, the readings assigned for the weekday are normally used. In certain cases, particularized readings are provided, that is to say, readings which highlight some particular aspect of the spiritual life or activity of the Saint. The use of such readings is not to be insisted upon, unless a pastoral reason truly suggests it.

358. In the Lectionary for weekdays, readings are provided for each day of every week throughout the entire course of the year; hence, these readings will in general be used on the days to which they are assigned, unless there occurs a Solemnity, a Feast, or Memorial that has its own New Testament readings, that is to say, readings in which mention is made of the Saint being celebrated.

Should, however, the continuous reading during the week from time to time be interrupted, on account of some Solemnity or Feast, or some particular celebration, then the Priest shall be permitted, bearing in mind the scheme of readings for the entire week, either to combine parts omitted with other readings or to decide which readings are to be given preference over others.

In Masses for special groups, the Priest shall be allowed to choose texts more particularly suited to the particular celebration, provided they are taken from the texts of an approved Lectionary.

359. In addition, in the Lectionary a special selection of texts from Sacred Scripture is given for Ritual Masses into which certain Sacraments or Sacramentals are incorporated, or for Masses that are celebrated for certain needs.

Sets of readings of this kind have been so prescribed so that through a more apt hearing of the Word of God the faithful may be led to a fuller understanding of the mystery in which they are participating, and may be educated to a more ardent love of the Word of God.

Therefore, the texts proclaimed in the celebration are to be chosen keeping in mind both an appropriate pastoral reason and the options allowed in this matter.

360. At times, a longer and shorter form of the same text is given. In choosing between these two forms, a pastoral criterion should be kept in mind. On such an occasion, attention should be paid to the capacity of the faithful to listen with fruit to a reading of greater or lesser length, and to their capacity to hear a more complete text, which is then explained in the Homily.[142]

---

[142] Missale Romanum, *Ordo lectionum Missae*, editio typica altera, 1981, Praenotanda, no. 80.

361. When a possibility is given of choosing between one or other text laid down, or suggested as optional, attention shall be paid to the good of participants, whether, that is to say, it is a matter of using an easier text or one more appropriate for a given gathering, or of repeating or setting aside a text that is assigned as proper to some particular celebration while being optional for another,[143] just as pastoral advantage may suggest.

Such a situation may arise either when the same text would have to be read again within a few days, as, for example, on a Sunday and on a subsequent weekday, or when it is feared that a certain text might give rise to some difficulties for a particular group of the Christian faithful. However, care should be taken that, when choosing scriptural passages, parts of Sacred Scripture are not permanently excluded.

362. In addition to the options noted above for choosing certain more suitable texts, the Conference of Bishops has the faculty, in particular circumstances, to indicate some adaptations as regards readings, provided that the texts are chosen from a duly approved Lectionary.

The Orations

363.   In any Mass the orations proper to that Mass are used, unless otherwise noted.

On Memorials of Saints, the proper Collect is said or, if this is lacking, one from an appropriate Common. As to the Prayer over the Offerings and the Prayer after Communion, unless these are proper, they may be taken either from the Common or from the weekday of the current time of year.

On the weekdays in Ordinary Time, however, besides the orations from the previous Sunday, orations from another Sunday in Ordinary Time may be used, or one of the Prayers for Various Needs provided in the Missal. However, it shall always be permissible to use from these Masses the Collect alone.

In this way a richer collection of texts is provided, by which the prayer life of the faithful is more abundantly nourished.

---

[143] *Ibidem,* no. 81.

However, during the more important times of the year, provision has already been made for this by means of the orations proper to these times of the year that exist for each weekday in the Missal.

The Eucharistic Prayer

364. The numerous Prefaces with which the Roman Missal is endowed have as their purpose to bring out more fully the motives for thanksgiving within the Eucharistic Prayer and to set out more clearly the different facets of the mystery of salvation.

365. The choice between the Eucharistic Prayers found in the Order of Mass is suitably guided by the following norms:

a) Eucharistic Prayer I, or the Roman Canon, which may always be used, is especially suited for use on days to which a proper text for the Communicantes (*In communion with those whose memory we venerate*) is assigned or in Masses endowed with a proper form of the Hanc igitur (*Therefore, Lord, we pray*) and also in the celebrations of the Apostles and of the Saints mentioned in the Prayer itself; likewise it is especially suited for use on Sundays, unless for pastoral reasons Eucharistic Prayer III is preferred.

b) Eucharistic Prayer II, on account of its particular features, is more appropriately used on weekdays or in special circumstances. Although it is provided with its own Preface, it may also be used with other Prefaces, especially those that sum up the mystery of salvation, for example, the Common Prefaces. When Mass is celebrated for a particular deceased person, the special formula given may be used at the proper point, namely, before the part *Remember also our brothers and sisters*.

c) Eucharistic Prayer III may be said with any Preface. Its use should be preferred on Sundays and festive days. If, however, this Eucharistic Prayer is used in Masses for the Dead, the special formula for a deceased person may be used, to be included at the proper place, namely after the words: *in your compassion, O merciful Father, gather to yourself all your children scattered throughout the world.*

d) Eucharistic Prayer IV has an invariable Preface and gives a fuller summary of salvation history. It may be used when a Mass has no Preface of its own and on Sundays in Ordinary Time. On account of its structure, no special formula for a deceased person may be inserted into this prayer.

The Chants

366.　It is not permitted to substitute other chants for those found in the Order of Mass, for example, at the Agnus Dei (*Lamb of God*).

367.　In choosing the chants between the readings, as well as the chants at the Entrance, at the Offertory, and at Communion, the norms laid down in their proper places are to be observed (*cf. nos. 40-41, 47-48, 61-64, 74, 86-88*).

Chapter VIII

MASSES AND PRAYERS FOR VARIOUS NEEDS AND OCCASIONS AND MASSES FOR THE DEAD

I. MASSES AND PRAYERS FOR VARIOUS NEEDS AND OCCASIONS

368. Since the liturgy of the Sacraments and Sacramentals has as its effect that for the faithful who are properly disposed almost every event in life is sanctified by the divine grace that flows from the Paschal Mystery,[144] and because the Eucharist is the Sacrament of Sacraments, the Missal provides examples of Mass formularies and orations that may be used in the various occasions of Christian life for the needs of the whole world or for the needs of the Church, whether universal or local.

369. In view of the rather broad possibilities of choice among the readings and orations, it is desirable that Masses for Various Needs and Occasions be used in moderation, that is, when truly required.

370. In all the Masses for Various Needs and Occasions, unless expressly indicated otherwise, it is permissible to use the weekday readings and also the chants between them, if they are suited to the celebration.

371. Among Masses of this kind are included Ritual Masses, Masses for Various Needs and Occasions and Votive Masses.

372. Ritual Masses are connected to the celebration of certain Sacraments or Sacramentals. They are prohibited on Sundays of Advent, Lent, and Easter, on Solemnities, on the days within the Octave of Easter, on the Commemoration of All the Faithful

---

[144] Cf. Second Ecumenical Council of the Vatican, Constitution on the Sacred Liturgy, *Sacrosanctum Concilium*, no. 61.

Departed (All Souls' Day), on Ash Wednesday, and during Holy Week, and furthermore due regard is to be had for the norms set out in the ritual books or in the Masses themselves.

373. Masses for Various Needs and Occasions are used in certain situations either as occasion arises or at fixed times. It is from these that Masses may be chosen by the competent authority for special days of prayer in the course of the year that are established by the Conference of Bishops.

374. If any case of a graver need or of pastoral advantage should arise, at the direction of the Diocesan Bishop or with his permission, an appropriate Mass may be celebrated on any day except Solemnities, the Sundays of Advent, Lent, and Easter, days within the Octave of Easter, the Commemoration of All the Faithful Departed (All Souls' Day), Ash Wednesday and the days of Holy Week.

375. Votive Masses of the mysteries of the Lord or in honour of the Blessed Virgin Mary or of the Angels or of any given Saint or of all the Saints may be said in response to the devotion of the faithful on weekdays in Ordinary Time, even if an Optional Memorial occurs. However, it is not permitted to celebrate as Votive Masses those that refer to mysteries related to events in the life of the Lord or of the Blessed Virgin Mary, with the exception of the Mass of the Immaculate Conception, since their celebration is an integral part of the course of the liturgical year.

376. On days when there occurs an Obligatory Memorial or on a weekday of Advent up to and including 16 December, of Christmas Time from 2 January, and of Easter Time after the Octave of Easter, Masses for Various Needs and Occasions and Votive Masses are in principle forbidden. If, however, some real necessity or pastoral advantage calls for it, in the estimation of the rector of the church or the Priest Celebrant himself, a Mass appropriate to the same may be used in a celebration with the people.

377. On weekdays in Ordinary Time when an Optional Memorial occurs or when the Office is of the weekday, it is permissible to celebrate any Mass for Various Needs and Occasions, or use any prayer for the same, but to the exclusion of Ritual Masses.

378. Particularly recommended is the Saturday commemoration of the Blessed Virgin Mary, because it is to the Mother of the Redeemer that in the Liturgy of the Church firstly and before all the Saints veneration is given.[145]

II. MASSES FOR THE DEAD

379. The Church offers the Eucharistic Sacrifice of Christ's Pasch for the dead so that, since all the members of Christ's Body are in communion with one another, what implores spiritual help for some, may bring comforting hope to others.

380. Among the Masses for the Dead, the Funeral Mass holds first place. It may be celebrated on any day except for Solemnities that are Holydays of Obligation, Thursday of Holy Week, the Paschal Triduum, and the Sundays of Advent, Lent, and Easter, with due regard also for all the other requirements of the norm of the law.[146]

381. A Mass for the Dead, on receiving the news of a death, for the final burial, or the first anniversary, may be celebrated even on days within the Octave of the Nativity of the Lord, on days when an Obligatory Memorial occurs, and on weekdays other than Ash Wednesday or the weekdays of Holy Week.

Other Masses for the Dead or 'daily' Masses, may be celebrated on weekdays in Ordinary Time on which Optional

---

[145] Cf. Second Ecumenical Council of the Vatican, Dogmatic Constitution on the Church, *Lumen gentium*, no. 54; Paul VI, Apostolic Exhortation, *Marialis cultus*, 2 February 1974, no. 9: *Acta Apostolicae Sedis* 66 (1974), pp. 122-123.

[146] Cf. particularly Code of Canon Law, *Codex Iuris Canonici*, cann. 1176-1185; Rituale Romanum, *Ordo Exsequiarum*, editio typica, 1969.

Memorials occur or when the Office is of the weekday, provided such Masses are actually applied for the dead.

382. At Funeral Masses there should usually be a short Homily, but to the exclusion of a funeral eulogy of any kind.

383. The faithful, and especially those of the deceased's family, should be urged to participate in the Eucharistic Sacrifice offered for the deceased person, also by receiving Holy Communion.

384. If the Funeral Mass is directly joined to the rite of burial, once the Prayer after Communion has been said and omitting the Concluding Rites, there takes place the Rite of Final Commendation or Farewell. This rite is celebrated only if the body is present.

385. In the arranging and choosing of the variable parts of the Mass for the Dead, especially the Funeral Mass (for example, orations, readings, and the Universal Prayer), pastoral considerations bearing upon the deceased, the family, and those attending should be kept in mind.

Moreover, pastors should take into special account those who are present at a liturgical celebration or who hear the Gospel on the occasion of the funeral and who may be non-Catholics or Catholics who never or hardly ever participate in the Eucharist or who seem even to have lost the faith. For Priests are ministers of Christ's Gospel for all.

CHAPTER IX

ADAPTATIONS WITHIN THE COMPETENCE OF BISHOPS AND BISHOPS' CONFERENCES

386. The renewal of the Roman Missal carried out in our time in accordance with the decrees of the Second Vatican Ecumenical Council has taken great care that all the faithful may display in the celebration of the Eucharist that full, conscious, and active participation that is required by the very nature of the Liturgy and to which the faithful, in virtue of their status as such, have a right and duty.[147]

However, in order that such a celebration may correspond all the more fully to the norms and the spirit of the Sacred Liturgy, certain further adaptations are set out in this Instruction and in the Order of Mass and entrusted to the judgement either of the Diocesan Bishop or of the Conferences of Bishops.

387. The Diocesan Bishop, who is to be regarded as the High Priest of his flock, from whom the life in Christ of his faithful in some sense derives and upon whom it depends,[148] must promote, regulate, and be vigilant over the liturgical life in his diocese. It is to him that in this Instruction is entrusted the regulating of the discipline of concelebration (*cf. nos. 202, 374*) and the establishing of norms regarding the function of serving the Priest at the altar (*cf. no. 107*), the distribution of Holy Communion under both kinds (*cf. no. 283*), and the construction and ordering of churches (*cf. no. 291*). It is above all for him, moreover, to nourish the spirit of the Sacred Liturgy in the Priests, Deacons, and faithful.

388. Those adaptations spoken of below that necessitate a wider degree of coordination are to be decided, in accord with the norm of law, in the Conference of Bishops.

---

[147] Cf. Second Ecumenical Council of the Vatican, Constitution on the Sacred Liturgy, *Sacrosanctum Concilium*, no. 14.

[148] Cf. *ibidem*, no. 41.

389. It is the competence, in the first place, of the Conferences of Bishops to prepare and approve an edition of this Roman Missal in the authorized vernacular languages, so that, once their decisions have been accorded the *recognitio* of the Apostolic See, the edition may be used in the regions to which it pertains.[149]

The Roman Missal, whether in Latin or in legitimately approved vernacular translations, is to be published in its entirety.

390. It is for the Conferences of Bishops to formulate the adaptations indicated in this General Instruction and in the Order of Mass and, once their decisions have been accorded the *recognitio* of the Apostolic See, to introduce them into the Missal itself. They are such as these:

– the gestures and bodily posture of the faithful (*cf. no. 43*);

– the gestures of veneration toward the altar and the Book of the Gospels (*cf. no. 273*);

– the texts of the chants at the Entrance, at the Presentation of the Gifts, and at Communion (*cf. nos. 48, 74, 87*);

– the readings from Sacred Scripture to be used in special circumstances (*cf. no. 362*);

– the form of the gesture of peace (*cf. no. 82*);

– the manner of receiving Holy Communion (*cf. nos. 160, 283*);

– the materials for the altar and sacred furnishings, especially the sacred vessels, and also the materials, form, and colour of the liturgical vestments (*cf. nos. 301, 326, 329, 339, 342-346*).

It shall be permissible for Directories or pastoral Instructions that the Conferences of Bishops judge useful to be included, with the prior *recognitio* of the Apostolic See, in the Roman Missal at an appropriate place.

---

[149] Cf. Code of Canon Law, *Codex Iuris Canonici*, can. 838 §3.

391. It is for the same Conferences of Bishops to attend to the translations of the biblical texts that are used in the celebration of Mass, exercising special care in this. For it is out of the Sacred Scripture that the readings are read and are explained in the Homily and that Psalms are sung, and it is by the influence of Sacred Scripture and at its prompting that prayers, orations, and liturgical chants are fashioned in such a way that it is from Sacred Scripture that actions and signs derive their meaning.[150]

Language should be used that corresponds to the capacity for understanding of the faithful and is suitable for public proclamation, while maintaining those characteristics that are proper to the different ways of speaking used in the biblical books.

392. It shall also be for Conferences of Bishops to prepare with care a translation of the other texts, so that, even though the character of each language is respected, the meaning of the original Latin text is fully and faithfully rendered. In accomplishing this task, it is desirable that the different literary genres used at Mass be taken into account, such as the presidential prayers, the antiphons, the acclamations, the responses, the litanies of supplication, and so on.

It should be borne in mind that the primary purpose of the translation of the texts is not for meditation, but rather for their proclamation or singing during an actual celebration.

Language should be used that is accommodated to the faithful of the region, but is noble and marked by literary quality, even though there will always be a necessity for some catechesis on the biblical and Christian meaning of certain words and expressions.

Moreover, it is preferable that in regions that share the same language, the same translation be used insofar as possible for liturgical texts, especially for biblical texts and for the Order of Mass.[151]

---

[150] Cf. Second Ecumenical Council of the Vatican, Constitution on the Sacred Liturgy, *Sacrosanctum Concilium*, no. 24.

[151] Cf. *ibidem*, no. 36 § 3.

393. Bearing in mind the important place that singing has in a celebration as a necessary or integral part of the Liturgy,[152] it is for the Conference of Bishops to approve suitable musical settings especially for the texts of the Ordinary of Mass, for the people's responses and acclamations and for the special rites that occur in the course of the liturgical year.

Likewise it is for the Conference to judge which musical forms, melodies, and musical instruments may be lawfully admitted into divine worship, insofar as these are truly suitable for sacred use, or can be made suitable.

In England and Wales: Bearing in mind the important place that singing has in a celebration as a necessary or integral part of the Liturgy, all musical settings of the texts of the Ordinary of Mass, for the people's responses and acclamations and for the special rites that occur in the course of the liturgical year must be submitted to the Conference of Bishops of England and Wales for review and approval prior to publication.

Likewise it is for the Conference to judge which musical forms, melodies, and musical instruments may be lawfully admitted into divine worship, insofar as these are truly suitable for sacred use, or can be made suitable.

In Scotland: Bearing in mind the important place that singing has in a celebration as a necessary or integral part of the Liturgy, all musical settings of the texts of the Ordinary of Mass, for the people's responses and acclamations and for the special rites that occur in the course of the liturgical year must be submitted to the Conference of Bishops of Scotland for review and approval prior to publication.

Likewise it is for the Conference to judge which musical forms, melodies, and musical instruments may be lawfully admitted into divine worship, insofar as these are truly suitable for sacred use, or can be made suitable.

[152] Cf. *ibidem*, no. 112.

394. Each diocese should have its own Calendar and Proper of Masses. For its part, the Conference of Bishops should draw up a proper Calendar for the nation or, together with other Conferences, a Calendar for a wider territory, to be approved by the Apostolic See.[153]

In carrying out this task, to the greatest extent possible the Lord's Day is to be preserved and safeguarded, as the primordial feast day, and hence other celebrations, unless they are truly of the greatest importance, should not have precedence over it.[154] Care should likewise be taken that the liturgical year as revised by decree of the Second Vatican Council not be obscured by secondary elements.

In the drawing up of the Calendar of a nation, the Rogation Days and Ember Days should be indicated (*cf. no. 373*), as well as the forms and texts for their celebration,[155] and other special measures should also be kept in mind.

It is appropriate that in publishing the Missal, celebrations proper to an entire nation or territory be inserted at the proper place among the celebrations of the General Calendar, while those proper to a region or diocese should have a place in a special appendix.

395. Finally, if the participation of the faithful and their spiritual welfare require variations and profounder adaptations in order for the sacred celebration to correspond with the culture and traditions of the different nations, then Conferences of Bishops may propose these to the Apostolic See in accordance with article 40 of the Constitution on the Sacred Liturgy for introduction with the Apostolic See's consent, especially in the case of nations to whom the Gospel has been more recently

---

[153] Cf. *Universal Norms on the Liturgical Year and the Calendar*, nos. 48-51, below, pp. 164-165; Sacred Congregation for Divine Worship, Instruction, *Calendaria particularia*, 24 June 1970, nos. 4, 8: *Acta Apostolicae Sedis* 62 (1970), pp. 652-653.

[154] Cf. Second Ecumenical Council of the Vatican, Constitution on the Sacred Liturgy, *Sacrosanctum Concilium*, no. 106.

[155] Cf. *Universal Norms on the Liturgical Year and the Calendar*, nos. 46, below, p. 163; Sacred Congregation for Divine Worship, Instruction, *Calendaria particularia*, 24 June 1970, no. 38: *Acta Apostolicae Sedis* 62 (1970), p. 660.

proclaimed.[156] The special norms handed down by means of the *Instruction on the Roman Liturgy and Inculturation*[157] should be attentively observed.

As regards the procedures in this matter, these should be observed:

Firstly, a detailed preliminary proposal should be set before the Apostolic See, so that, after the necessary faculty has been granted, the detailed working out of the individual points of adaptation may proceed.

Once these proposals have been duly approved by the Apostolic See, experiments should be carried out for specified periods and at specified places. When the period of experimentation is concluded, the Conference of Bishops shall decide, if the case requires, upon pursuing the adaptations and shall submit a mature formulation of the matter to the judgement of the Apostolic See.[158]

396. However, before proceeding to new adaptations, especially profounder ones, great care shall be taken to promote due instruction of the clergy and the faithful in a wise and orderly manner, so as to take advantage of the faculties already foreseen and to apply fully the pastoral norms in keeping with the spirit of the celebration.

397. The principle shall moreover be respected, according to which each particular Church must be in accord with the universal Church not only regarding the doctrine of the faith and sacramental signs, but also as to the usages universally received from apostolic and unbroken tradition. These are to be kept not only so that errors may be avoided, but also so that the faith may be handed on in its integrity, since the

---

[156] Cf. Second Ecumenical Council of the Vatican, Constitution on the Sacred Liturgy, *Sacrosanctum Concilium*, nos. 37-40.

[157] Cf. Congregation for Divine Worship and the Discipline of the Sacraments, Instruction, *Varietates legitimae*, 25 January 1994, nos. 54, 62-69: *Acta Apostolicae Sedis* 87 (1995), pp. 308-309, 311-313.

[158] Cf. *ibidem*, nos. 66-68: *Acta Apostolicae Sedis* 87 (1995), p. 313.

Church's rule of prayer (*lex orandi*) corresponds to her rule of faith (*lex credendi*).[159]

The Roman Rite constitutes a notable and precious part of the liturgical treasure and patrimony of the Catholic Church; its riches are conducive to the good of the universal Church, so that their loss would gravely harm her.

This Rite has in the course of the centuries not only preserved the liturgical usages that arose in the city of Rome, but has also in a deep, organic, and harmonious way integrated into itself certain other usages derived from the customs and culture of different peoples and of various particular Churches whether of the West or the East, so acquiring a certain supra-regional character. As to our own times, the identity and unitary expression of this Rite is found in the typical editions of the liturgical books promulgated by authority of the Supreme Pontiff, and in the liturgical books corresponding to them approved for their territories by the Conferences of Bishops and endowed with the *recognitio* of the Apostolic See.[160]

398. The norm established by the Second Vatican Council, namely that in the liturgical renewal innovations should not be made unless required by true and certain usefulness to the Church, nor without exercising caution to ensure that new forms grow in some sense organically from forms already existing,[161] must also be applied to implementation of the inculturation of the Roman Rite as such.[162] Inculturation, moreover, requires a necessary length of time, lest the authentic liturgical tradition suffer hasty and incautious contamination.

---

[159] Cf. *ibidem,* nos. 26-27: *Acta Apostolicae Sedis* 87 (1995), pp. 298-299.

[160] Cf. John Paul II, Apostolic Letter, *Vicesimus quintus annus,* 4 December 1988, no. 16: *Acta Apostolicae Sedis* 81 (1989), p. 912; Congregation for Divine Worship and the Discipline of the Sacraments, Instruction, *Varietates legitimae,* 25 January 1994, nos. 2, 36: *Acta Apostolicae Sedis* 87 (1995), pp. 288, 302.

[161] Cf. Second Ecumenical Council of the Vatican, Constitution on the Sacred Liturgy, *Sacrosanctum Concilium,* no. 23.

[162] Cf. Congregation for Divine Worship and the Discipline of the Sacraments, Instruction, *Varietates legitimae,* 25 January 1994, no. 46: *Acta Apostolicae Sedis* 87 (1995), p. 306.

Finally, the pursuit of inculturation does not have as its purpose in any way the creation of new families of rites, but aims rather at meeting the needs of a particular culture, though in such a way that adaptations introduced either into the Missal or coordinated with other liturgical books are not at variance with the proper character of the Roman Rite.[163]

399. And so, the Roman Missal, though in a diversity of languages and with some variety of customs,[164] must in the future be safeguarded as an instrument and an outstanding sign of the integrity and unity of the Roman Rite.[165]

---

[163] Cf. *ibidem*, no. 36: *Acta Apostolicae Sedis* 87 (1995), p. 302.

[164] Cf. *ibidem*, no. 54: *Acta Apostolicae Sedis* 87 (1995), pp. 308-309.

[165] Cf. Second Ecumenical Council of the Vatican, Constitution on the Sacred Liturgy, *Sacrosanctum Concilium*, no. 38; Paul VI, Apostolic Constitution, *Missale Romanum*, above, p. 19.

UNIVERSAL NORMS
FOR THE LITURGICAL YEAR
AND THE
GENERAL ROMAN CALENDAR

APOSTOLIC LETTER
MOTU PROPRIO

APPROVAL OF THE UNIVERSAL NORMS ON THE LITURGICAL YEAR AND THE NEW GENERAL ROMAN CALENDAR

POPE PAUL VI

The Paschal Mystery's celebration is of supreme importance in Christian worship, as we are clearly taught by the sacred Second Vatican Council, and its meaning is unfolded over the course of days, of weeks, and of the whole year. From this it follows that it is necessary that this same Paschal Mystery of Christ be placed in clearer light in the reform of the liturgical year, for which norms were given by the Sacred Synod itself, with regard at once to the arrangement of what is known as the Proper of Time and of the Proper of Saints and to the revision of the Roman Calendar.[166]

I

For in fact, with the passage of centuries, it has happened that, partly from the increase in the number of vigils, religious festivals and their extension over an octave, and partly from the gradual introduction of new elements into the liturgical year, the Christian faithful had come not rarely to practise particular pious exercises in such a way that their minds seemed to have become somewhat distracted from the principal mysteries of divine redemption.

Yet everybody knows that several decisions were issued by Our Predecessors Saint Pius X and John XXIII, of blessed memory, with the intention on the one hand that Sunday, restored to its original dignity, should be truly considered by

---

[166] Cf. Second Vatican Council, Constitution on the Sacred Liturgy, *Sacrosanctum Concilium*, nos. 102-111.

all as 'the primordial feast day',[167] and on the other that the liturgical celebration of Holy Lent should be restored. It is no less true that Our Predecessor Pius XII, of blessed memory, ordered by means of a decree[168] that in the Western Church during Easter Night the solemn vigil be restored, so that during it the People of God might renew their spiritual covenant with Christ the risen Lord in the course of celebrating the Sacraments of Christian Initiation.

That is to say, these Supreme Pontiffs, following the teaching of the holy Fathers and holding firmly to the doctrine handed down by the Catholic Church, rightly considered not only that in the course of the liturgical year those deeds are commemorated by means of which Christ Jesus in dying brought us salvation, and the memory of past actions is recalled, so that the Christian faithful, even the more simple of them, may receive spiritual instruction and nourishment, but these Popes also taught that the celebration of the liturgical year 'possesses a distinct sacramental power and efficacy to strengthen Christian life'.[169] This is also Our own mind and teaching.

Rightly and properly, therefore, as we celebrate the 'mystery of the Nativity of Christ'[170] and his appearance in the world, we pray that 'we may be inwardly transformed through him whom we recognize as outwardly like ourselves',[171] and that while we celebrate Christ's Pasch, we ask almighty God that those who have been reborn with Christ may 'hold fast in their lives to the Sacrament they have received in faith'.[172] For, in the words of the Second Vatican Council, 'honouring thus the mysteries of redemption, the Church opens to the faithful the riches of her

---

[167] Cf. *ibidem*, no. 106.

[168] Cf. Sacred Congregation of Rites, Decree, *Dominicae Resurrectionis*, 9 February 1951: *Acta Apostolicae Sedis* 43 (1951), pp. 128-129.

[169] Sacred Congregation of Rites, General Decree, *Maxima redemptionis nostrae mysteria*, 16 November 1955: *Acta Apostolicae Sedis* 47 (1955), p. 839.

[170] St Leo the Great, *Sermo XXVII in Nativitate Domini* 7, 1: PL 54, 216.

[171] Cf. *Missale Romanum* [*editio typica*, 1962], Epiphany, oration [Collect 2 for the Baptism of the Lord, below, p. 227].

[172] Cf. *Missale Romanum* [*editio typica*, 1962], Tuesday of Easter Week, oration [Collect of Monday within the Octave of Easter, below, p. 426].

Lord's powers and merits, so that these are in some way made present in every age in order that the faithful may touch them and be filled with the grace of salvation.'[173]

Hence the purpose of the revision of the liturgical year and of the norms accomplishing its reform, is nothing other than that through faith, hope, and charity the faithful may share more deeply in 'the whole mystery of Christ, unfolded through the cycle of the year'.[174]

II

We see no contradiction between what has already been said and the clear brightness that shines from the feasts of the Blessed Virgin Mary, 'who is joined by an inseparable bond to the saving work of her Son',[175] and the Memorials of the Saints, to which the birthdays of 'our Lords the Martyrs and Victors'[176] are rightly joined, since 'the feasts of the Saints proclaim the wonderful works of Christ in his servants and offer the faithful fitting examples for their imitation'.[177] Furthermore, the Catholic Church has always held firmly and with assurance that in the feasts of the Saints the Paschal Mystery of Christ is proclaimed and renewed.[178]

Therefore, since it cannot be denied that with the passage of centuries more feasts of the Saints were introduced than was appropriate, the Sacred Synod duly cautioned: 'Lest the feasts of the Saints take precedence over the feasts commemorating the very mysteries of salvation, many of them should be left to be celebrated by a particular Church or nation or religious family;

---

[173] Second Vatican Council, Constitution on the Sacred Liturgy, *Sacrosanctum Concilium*, no. 102.

[174] Cf. *ibidem*, no. 102.

[175] *Ibidem*, no. 103.

[176] Cf. B. Mariani, editor, *Breviarium Syriacum* (5th century), Rome 1956, p. 27.

[177] Cf. Second Vatican Council, Constitution on the Sacred Liturgy, *Sacrosanctum Concilium*, no. 111.

[178] Cf. *ibidem*, no. 104.

and only those should be extended to the Universal Church that commemorate Saints having universal importance'.[179]

Furthermore, to put these decrees of the Ecumenical Council into effect, the names of some Saints have been removed from the General Calendar, and likewise permission has been granted for the observation of the Memorials of some other Saints to be made optional, and that their cult be appropriately restored to their own regions. As a result, the removal from the Roman Calendar of the names of certain Saints not known throughout the world has allowed the addition of names of some Martyrs from regions to which the announcement of the Gospel spread in later times. Thus the single catalogue displays in equal dignity, as representatives of all peoples, as it were, some who either shed their blood for Christ or were outstanding in their most signal virtues.

For these reasons we regard the new General Calendar drawn up for use in the Latin Rite as being more in keeping with the spiritual attitudes and sentiments of these times and to be a clearer reflection of that characteristic of the Church which is her universality, since it proposes henceforth names of outstanding men to put before the whole People of God clear examples of holiness, developed in many different ways. There is no need to speak of the immense spiritual value of this for the whole multitude of Christians.

Therefore, after most carefully pondering all these matters before the Lord, with Our Apostolic Authority We approve the new General Roman Calendar drawn up by the Consilium for the Implementation of the Constitution on the Sacred Liturgy and likewise the universal norms governing the ordering of the liturgical year, so that they may come into force on the first day of the month of January in the coming year, 1970, in accordance with the decrees that the Sacred Congregation of Rites has prepared in conjunction with the aforementioned Consilium, which are to remain in force until the publication of the duly renewed Roman Missal and Breviary.

---

[179] Cf. *ibidem*, no. 111.

Whatsoever we have laid down *motu proprio* in these Our Letters we order to be held firm and valid, notwithstanding, to the extent necessary, the Constitutions and Apostolic Ordinances issued by Our Predecessors, or other prescriptions worthy of mention and derogation.

Given in Rome, at Saint Peter's, on the fourteenth day of the month of February in the year 1969, the sixth of Our Pontificate.

PAUL VI, POPE

UNIVERSAL NORMS ON THE LITURGICAL YEAR AND THE CALENDAR

CHAPTER I

THE LITURGICAL YEAR

1.   Holy Church celebrates the saving work of Christ on prescribed days in the course of the year with sacred remembrance. Each week, on the day called the Lord's Day, she commemorates the Resurrection of the Lord, which she also celebrates once a year in the great Paschal Solemnity, together with his blessed Passion. In fact, throughout the course of the year the Church unfolds the entire mystery of Christ and observes the birthdays of the Saints.

During the different periods of the liturgical year, in accord with traditional discipline, the Church completes the education of the faithful by means of both spiritual and bodily devotional practices, instruction, prayer, works of penance and works of mercy.[180]

2.   The principles that follow can and must be applied both to the Roman Rite and all other Rites; however, the practical norms are to be understood as applying solely to the Roman Rite, except in the case of those that by their very nature also affect the other Rites.[181]

TITLE I – THE LITURGICAL DAYS

I. The Liturgical Day in General

3.   Each and every day is sanctified by the liturgical celebrations of the People of God, especially by the Eucharistic Sacrifice and the Divine Office.

---

[180] Cf. Second Vatican Council, Constitution on the Sacred Liturgy, *Sacrosanctum Concilium*, nos. 102-105.

[181] Cf. *ibidem*, no. 3.

The liturgical day runs from midnight to midnight. However, the celebration of Sunday and of Solemnities begins already on the evening of the previous day.

II. Sunday

4.   On the first day of each week, which is known as the Day of the Lord or the Lord's Day, the Church, by an apostolic tradition that draws its origin from the very day of the Resurrection of Christ, celebrates the Paschal Mystery. Hence, Sunday must be considered the primordial feast day.[182]

5.   Because of its special importance, the celebration of Sunday gives way only to Solemnities and Feasts of the Lord; indeed, the Sundays of Advent, Lent and Easter have precedence over all Feasts of the Lord and over all Solemnities. In fact, Solemnities occurring on these Sundays are transferred to the following Monday unless they occur on Palm Sunday or on Sunday of the Lord's Resurrection.

6.   Sunday excludes in principle the permanent assigning of any other celebration. However:

a) the Sunday within the Octave of the Nativity is the Feast of the Holy Family;

b) the Sunday following 6 January is the Feast of the Baptism of the Lord;

c) the Sunday after Pentecost is the Solemnity of the Most Holy Trinity;

d) the Last Sunday in Ordinary Time is the Solemnity of Our Lord Jesus Christ, King of the Universe.

7.   Where the Solemnities of the Epiphany, the Ascension and the Most Holy Body and Blood of Christ are not observed as Holydays of Obligation, they should be assigned to a Sunday as their proper day in this manner:

a) the Epiphany is assigned to the Sunday that falls between 2 January and 8 January;

---

[182] Cf. *ibidem*, no. 106.

b) the Ascension to the Seventh Sunday of Easter;

c) the Solemnity of the Most Holy Body and Blood of Christ to the Sunday after Trinity Sunday.

III. Solemnities, Feasts, and Memorials

8. In the cycle of the year, as she celebrates the mystery of Christ, the Church also venerates with a particular love the Blessed Mother of God, Mary, and proposes to the devotion of the faithful the Memorials of the Martyrs and other Saints.[183]

9. The Saints who have universal importance are celebrated in an obligatory way throughout the whole Church; other Saints are either inscribed in the calendar, but for optional celebration, or are left to be honoured by a particular Church, or nation, or religious family.[184]

10. Celebrations, according to the importance assigned to them, are hence distinguished one from another and termed: Solemnity, Feast, Memorial.

11. Solemnities are counted among the most important days, whose celebration begins with First Vespers (Evening Prayer I) on the preceding day. Some Solemnities are also endowed with their own Vigil Mass, which is to be used on the evening of the preceding day, if an evening Mass is celebrated.

12. The celebration of the two greatest Solemnities, Easter and the Nativity, is extended over eight days. Each Octave is governed by its own rules.

13. Feasts are celebrated within the limits of the natural day; accordingly they have no First Vespers (Evening Prayer I), except in the case of Feasts of the Lord that fall on a Sunday in Ordinary Time or in Christmas Time and which replace the Sunday Office.

---

[183] Cf. *ibidem*, nos. 103-104.

[184] Cf. *ibidem*, no. 111.

14.　　Memorials are either obligatory or optional; their observance is integrated into the celebration of the occurring weekday in accordance with the norms set forth in the General Instruction of the Roman Missal and of the Liturgy of the Hours.

Obligatory Memorials which fall on weekdays of Lent may only be celebrated as Optional Memorials.

If several Optional Memorials are inscribed in the Calendar on the same day, only one may be celebrated, the others being omitted.

15.　　On Saturdays in Ordinary Time when no Obligatory Memorial occurs, an Optional Memorial of the Blessed Virgin Mary may be celebrated.

IV. Weekdays

16.　　The days of the week that follow Sunday are called weekdays; however, they are celebrated differently according to the importance of each.

a) Ash Wednesday and the weekdays of Holy Week, from Monday up to and including Thursday, take precedence over all other celebrations.

b) The weekdays of Advent from 17 December up to and including 24 December and all the weekdays of Lent have precedence over Obligatory Memorials.

c) Other weekdays give way to all Solemnities and Feasts and are combined with Memorials.

TITLE II – THE CYCLE OF THE YEAR

17.　　Over the course of the year the Church celebrates the whole mystery of Christ, from the Incarnation to Pentecost Day and the days of waiting for the Advent of the Lord.[185]

---

[185] Cf. *ibidem*, no. 102.

I. The Paschal Triduum

18.　Since Christ accomplished his work of human redemption and of the perfect glorification of God principally through his Paschal Mystery, in which by dying he has destroyed our death, and by rising restored our life, the sacred Paschal Triduum of the Passion and Resurrection of the Lord shines forth as the high point of the entire liturgical year.[186] Therefore the pre-eminence that Sunday has in the week, the Solemnity of Easter has in the liturgical year.[187]

19.　The Paschal Triduum of the Passion and Resurrection of the Lord begins with the evening Mass of the Lord's Supper, has its centre in the Easter Vigil, and closes with Vespers (Evening Prayer) of the Sunday of the Resurrection.

20.　On Friday of the Passion of the Lord[188] and, if appropriate, also on Holy Saturday until the Easter Vigil,[189] the sacred Paschal Fast is everywhere observed.

21.　The Easter Vigil, in the holy night when the Lord rose again, is considered the 'mother of all holy Vigils',[190] in which the Church, keeping watch, awaits the Resurrection of Christ and celebrates it in the Sacraments. Therefore, the entire celebration of this sacred Vigil must take place at night, so that it both begins after nightfall and ends before the dawn on the Sunday.

II. Easter Time

22.　The fifty days from the Sunday of the Resurrection to Pentecost Sunday are celebrated in joy and exultation as one feast day, indeed as one 'great Sunday'.[191]

---

[186] Cf. *ibidem*, no. 5.

[187] Cf. *ibidem*, no. 106.

[188] Cf. Paul VI, Apostolic Constitution, *Paenitemini*, 17 February 1966, II § 3: *Acta Apostolicae Sedis* 58 (1966), p. 184.

[189] Cf. Second Vatican Council, Constitution on the Sacred Liturgy, *Sacrosanctum Concilium*, no. 110.

[190] St Augustine, *Sermo* 219: PL 38, 1088.

[191] St Athanasius, *Epistula festalis* I: PG 26, 1366.

These are the days above all others in which the *Alleluia* is sung.

23.   The Sundays of this time of year are considered to be Sundays of Easter and are called, after Easter Sunday itself, the Second, Third, Fourth, Fifth, Sixth, and Seventh Sundays of Easter. This sacred period of fifty days concludes with Pentecost Sunday.

24.   The first eight days of Easter Time constitute the Octave of Easter and are celebrated as Solemnities of the Lord.

25.   On the fortieth day after Easter the Ascension of the Lord is celebrated, except where, not being observed as a Holyday of Obligation, it has been assigned to the Seventh Sunday of Easter (*cf. no. 7*).

26.   The weekdays from the Ascension up to and including the Saturday before Pentecost prepare for the coming of the Holy Spirit, the Paraclete.

III. Lent

27.   Lent is ordered to preparing for the celebration of Easter, since the Lenten liturgy prepares for celebration of the Paschal Mystery both catechumens, by the various stages of Christian Initiation, and the faithful, who recall their own Baptism and do penance.[192]

28.   The forty days of Lent run from Ash Wednesday up to but excluding the Mass of the Lord's Supper exclusive. From the beginning of Lent until the Paschal Vigil, the *Alleluia* is not said.

29.   On Ash Wednesday, the beginning of Lent, which is observed everywhere as a fast day,[193] ashes are distributed.

---

[192] Cf. Second Vatican Council, Constitution on the Sacred Liturgy, *Sacrosanctum Concilium*, no. 109.

[193] Cf. Paul VI, Apostolic Constitution, *Paenitemini*, 17 February 1966, II § 3: *Acta Apostolicae Sedis* 58 (1966), p. 184.

30.   The Sundays of this time of year are called the First, Second, Third, Fourth, and Fifth Sundays of Lent. The Sixth Sunday, on which Holy Week begins, is called, 'Palm Sunday of the Passion of the Lord'.

31.   Holy Week is ordered to the commemoration of Christ's Passion, beginning with his Messianic entrance into Jerusalem.

On Thursday of Holy Week, in the morning, the Bishop concelebrates Mass with his presbyterate and blesses the holy oils and consecrates the chrism.

IV. Christmas Time

32.   After the annual celebration of the Paschal Mystery, the Church has no more ancient custom than celebrating the memorial of the Nativity of the Lord and of his first manifestations, and this takes place in Christmas Time.

33.   Christmas Time runs from First Vespers (Evening Prayer I) of the Nativity of the Lord up to and including the Sunday after Epiphany or after 6 January.

34.   The Vigil Mass of the Nativity is used on the evening of 24 December, either before or after First Vespers (Evening Prayer I).

On the day of the Nativity of the Lord, following ancient Roman tradition, Mass may be celebrated three times, that is, in the night, at dawn and during the day.

35.   The Nativity of the Lord has its own Octave, arranged thus:

a) Sunday within the Octave or, if there is no Sunday, 30 December, is the Feast of the Holy Family of Jesus, Mary, and Joseph;

b) 26 December is the Feast of Saint Stephen, the First Martyr;

c) 27 December is the Feast of Saint John, Apostle and Evangelist;

d) 28 December is the Feast of the Holy Innocents;

e) 29, 30, and 31 December are days within the Octave;

f) 1 January, the Octave Day of the Nativity of the Lord, is the Solemnity of Mary, the Holy Mother of God, and also the commemoration of the conferral of the Most Holy Name of Jesus.

36.   The Sunday falling between 2 January and 5 January is the Second Sunday after the Nativity.

37.   The Epiphany of the Lord is celebrated on 6 January, unless, where it is not observed as a Holyday of Obligation, it has been assigned to the Sunday occurring between 2 and 8 January (*cf. no. 7*).

38.   The Sunday falling after 6 January is the Feast of the Baptism of the Lord.

V. Advent

39.   Advent has a twofold character, for it is a time of preparation for the Solemnities of Christmas, in which the First Coming of the Son of God to humanity is remembered, and likewise a time when, by remembrance of this, minds and hearts are led to look forward to Christ's Second Coming at the end of time. For these two reasons, Advent is a period of devout and expectant delight.

40.   Advent begins with First Vespers (Evening Prayer I) of the Sunday that falls on or closest to 30 November and it ends before First Vespers (Evening Prayer I) of Christmas.

41.   The Sundays of this time of year are named the First, Second, Third, and Fourth Sundays of Advent.

42.   The weekdays from 17 December up to and including 24 December are ordered in a more direct way to preparing for the Nativity of the Lord.

VI. Ordinary Time

43.   Besides the times of year that have their own distinctive character, there remain in the yearly cycle thirty-three or thirty-

four weeks in which no particular aspect of the mystery of Christ is celebrated, but rather the mystery of Christ itself is honoured in its fullness, especially on Sundays. This period is known as Ordinary Time.

44.   Ordinary Time begins on the Monday which follows the Sunday occurring after 6 January and extends up to and including the Tuesday before the beginning of Lent; it begins again on the Monday after Pentecost Sunday and ends before First Vespers (Evening Prayer I) of the First Sunday of Advent.

During these times of the year there is used the series of formularies given for the Sundays and weekdays of this time both in the Missal and in the Liturgy of the Hours (Vol. III-IV).

VII. Rogation Days and Ember Days

45.   On Rogation and Ember Days the Church is accustomed to entreat the Lord for the various needs of humanity, especially for the fruits of the earth and for human labour, and to give thanks to him publicly.

46.   In order that the Rogation Days and Ember Days may be adapted to the different regions and different needs of the faithful, the Conferences of Bishops should arrange the time and manner in which they are held.

Consequently, concerning their duration, whether they are to last one or more days, or be repeated in the course of the year, norms are to be established by the competent authority, taking into consideration local needs.

47.   The Mass for each day of these celebrations should be chosen from among the Masses for Various Needs, and should be one which is more particularly appropriate to the purpose of the supplications.

Chapter II

THE CALENDAR

Title I – The Calendar
and Celebrations to Be Inscribed in it

48. The ordering of the celebration of the liturgical year is governed by a calendar, which is either general or particular, depending on whether it has been laid down for the use of the entire Roman Rite, or for the use of a Particular Church or religious family.

49. In the General Calendar is inscribed both the entire cycle of celebrations of the mystery of salvation in the Proper of Time, and that of those Saints who have universal significance and therefore are obligatorily celebrated by everyone, and of other Saints who demonstrate the universality and continuity of sainthood within the People of God.

Particular calendars, on the other hand, contain celebrations of a more proper character, appropriately combined organically with the general cycle.[194] For individual Churches or religious families show special honour to those Saints who are proper to them for some particular reason.

Particular calendars, however, are to be drawn up by the competent authority and approved by the Apostolic See.

50. In drawing up a particular calendar, attention should be paid to the following:

a) The Proper of Time, that is, the cycle of Times, Solemnities, and Feasts by which the mystery of redemption is unfolded and honoured during the liturgical year, must always be kept intact and enjoy its rightful pre-eminence over particular celebrations.

---

[194] Cf. Sacred Congregation for Divine Worship, Instruction, *Calendaria particularia*, 24 June 1970: *Acta Apostolicae Sedis* 62 (1970), pp. 651-663.

b) Proper celebrations must be combined organically with universal celebrations, with attention to the rank and precedence indicated for each in the Table of Liturgical Days. So that particular calendars may not be overburdened, individual Saints should have only one celebration in the course of the liturgical year, although, where pastoral reasons recommend it, there may be another celebration in the form of an Optional Memorial marking the *translatio* or *inventio* of the bodies of Patron Saints or Founders of Churches or of religious families.

c) Celebrations granted by indult should not duplicate other celebrations already occurring in the cycle of the mystery of salvation, nor should their number be increased out of proportion.

51.   Although it is appropriate for each diocese to have its own Calendar and Proper for the Office and Mass, there is nevertheless nothing to prevent entire provinces, regions, nations, or even larger areas, having Calendars and Propers in common, prepared by cooperation among all concerned.

This principle may also be similarly observed in the case of religious calendars for several provinces under the same civil jurisdiction.

52.   A particular calendar is prepared by the insertion in the General Calendar of proper Solemnities, Feasts and Memorials, that is:

a) in a diocesan calendar, besides celebrations of Patrons and of the dedication of the cathedral church, the Saints and Blessed who have special connections with the diocese, e.g., by their birth, residence over a long period, or their death;

b) in a religious calendar, besides celebrations of the Title, the Founder and the Patron, those Saints and Blessed who were members of that religious family or had a special relationship with it;

c) in calendars for individual churches, besides the proper celebrations of the diocese or religious family, celebrations proper to the church that are listed in the Table of Liturgical

165

Days, and Saints whose body is kept in the church. Members of religious families, too, join the community of the local Church in celebrating the anniversary of the dedication of the cathedral church and the principal Patrons of the place and of the wider region where they live.

53.   When a diocese or religious family has the distinction of having many Saints and Blessed, care must be taken so that the calendar of the entire diocese or entire institute does not become overburdened. Consequently:

a) A common celebration can, first of all, be held of all the Saints and Blessed of a diocese or religious family, or of some category among them.

b) Only the Saints and Blessed of particular significance for the entire diocese or the entire religious family should be inscribed in the calendar as an individual celebration.

c) The other Saints or Blessed should be celebrated only in those places with which they have closer ties or where their bodies are kept.

54.   Proper celebrations should be inscribed in the Calendar as Obligatory or Optional Memorials, unless other provisions have been made for them in the Table of Liturgical Days, or there are special historical or pastoral reasons. There is no reason, however, why some celebrations may not be observed in certain places with greater solemnity than in the rest of the diocese or religious family.

55.   Celebrations inscribed in a particular calendar must be observed by all who are bound to follow that calendar and may only be removed from the calendar or changed in rank with the approval of the Apostolic See.

Title II – The Proper Day for Celebrations

56.   The Church's practice has been to celebrate the Saints on their 'birthday', a practice that it is appropriate to follow when proper celebrations are inscribed in particular calendars.

However, even though proper celebrations have special importance for individual particular Churches or individual religious families, it is greatly expedient that there be as much unity as possible in the celebration of Solemnities, Feasts and Obligatory Memorials inscribed in the General Calendar.

Consequently in inscribing proper celebrations in a particular calendar, the following should be observed:

a) Celebrations that are also listed in the General Calendar are to be inscribed on the same date in a particular calendar, with a change if necessary in the rank of celebration.

The same must be observed with regard to a diocesan or religious calendar for the inscription of celebrations proper to a single church.

b) Celebrations of Saints not found in the General Calendar should be assigned to their 'birthday'. If this is not known, the celebrations should be assigned to a date proper to the Saint for some other reason, e.g., the date of ordination or of the *inventio* or *translatio* of the Saint's body; otherwise to a day that is free from other celebrations in the particular Calendar.

c) If, on the other hand, the 'birthday' or other proper day is impeded by another obligatory celebration, even of lower rank, in the General Calendar or in a particular calendar, the celebration should be assigned to the closest date not so impeded.

d) However, if it is a question of celebrations that for pastoral reasons cannot be transferred to another date, the impeding celebration must itself be transferred.

e) Other celebrations, termed celebrations by indult, should be inscribed on a date more pastorally appropriate.

f) In order that the cycle of the liturgical year shine forth in all its clarity, but that the celebration of the Saints not be permanently impeded, dates that usually fall during Lent and the Octave of Easter, as well as the weekdays from 17 December to 31 December, should remain free of any particular celebration, unless it is a question of Obligatory Memorials, of Feasts found in the Table of Liturgical Days under no. 8: a, b, c, d, or of Solemnities that cannot be transferred to another time of the year.

The Solemnity of Saint Joseph, where it is observed as a Holyday of Obligation, should it fall on Palm Sunday of the Lord's Passion, is anticipated on the preceding Saturday, 18 March. Where, on the other hand, it is not observed as a Holyday of Obligation, it may be transferred by the Conference of Bishops to another day outside Lent.

57.   If any Saints or Blessed are inscribed together in the Calendar, they are always celebrated together, whenever their celebrations are of equal rank, even though one or more of them may be more proper. If, however, the celebration of one or more of these Saints or Blessed is of a higher rank, the Office of this or those Saints or Blessed alone is celebrated and the celebration of the others is omitted, unless it is appropriate to assign them to another date in the form of an Obligatory Memorial.

58.   For the pastoral good of the faithful, it is permitted to observe on Sundays in Ordinary Time those celebrations that fall during the week and that are agreeable to the devotion of the faithful, provided the celebrations rank above that Sunday in the Table of Liturgical Days. The Mass of such celebrations may be used at all the celebrations of Mass at which the people are present.

59.   Precedence among liturgical days, as regards their celebration, is governed solely by the following Table.

Table of Liturgical Days

according to their order of precedence

I

1. The Paschal Triduum of the Passion and Resurrection of the Lord.

2. The Nativity of the Lord, the Epiphany, the Ascension, and Pentecost.

   Sundays of Advent, Lent, and Easter.

   Ash Wednesday.

   Weekdays of Holy Week from Monday up to and including Thursday.

   Days within the Octave of Easter.

3. Solemnities inscribed in the General Calendar, whether of the Lord, of the Blessed Virgin Mary or of Saints.

   The Commemoration of All the Faithful Departed.

4. Proper Solemnities, namely:

   a) The Solemnity of the principal Patron of the place, city or state.

   b) The Solemnity of the dedication and of the anniversary of the dedication of one's own church.

   c) The Solemnity of the Title of one's own church.

   d) The Solemnity either of the Title
      or of the Founder
      or of the principal Patron of an Order or Congregation.

II

5. Feasts of the Lord inscribed in the General Calendar.

6. Sundays of Christmas Time and the Sundays in Ordinary Time.

169

7. Feasts of the Blessed Virgin Mary and of the Saints in the General Calendar.

8. Proper Feasts, namely:

    a) The Feast of the principal Patron of the diocese.

    b) The Feast of the anniversary of the dedication of the cathedral church.

    c) The Feast of the principal Patron of a region or province, or a country, or of a wider territory.

    d) The Feast of the Title, Founder, or principal Patron of an Order or Congregation and of a religious province, without prejudice to the prescriptions given under no. 4.

    e) Other Feasts proper to an individual church.

    f) Other Feasts inscribed in the Calendar of each diocese or Order or Congregation.

9. Weekdays of Advent from 17 December up to and including 24 December.

    Days within the Octave of Christmas.

    Weekdays of Lent.

III

10. Obligatory Memorials in the General Calendar.

11. Proper Obligatory Memorials, namely:

    a) The Memorial of a secondary Patron of the place, diocese, region, or religious province.

    b) Other Obligatory Memorials inscribed in the Calendar of each diocese, or Order or Congregation.

12. Optional Memorials, which, however, may be celebrated, in the special manner described in the *General Instruction of the Roman Missal* and of the Liturgy of the Hours, even on the days listed in no. 9.

In the same manner Obligatory Memorials may be celebrated as Optional Memorials if they happen to fall on Lenten weekdays.

13. Weekdays of Advent up to and including 16 December.

Weekdays of Christmas Time from 2 January until the Saturday after the Epiphany.

Weekdays of the Easter Time from Monday after the Octave of Easter up to and including the Saturday before Pentecost.

Weekdays in Ordinary Time.

60.   If several celebrations fall on the same day, the one that holds the highest rank according to the Table of Liturgical Days is observed. However, a Solemnity impeded by a liturgical day that takes precedence over it should be transferred to the closest day not listed under nos. 1-8 in the Table of Precedence, provided that what is laid down in no. 5 is observed. As to the Solemnity of the Annunciation of the Lord, whenever it falls on any day of Holy Week, it shall always be transferred to the Monday after the Second Sunday of Easter.

Other celebrations are omitted in that year.

61.   Should on the other hand, Vespers (Evening Prayer) of the current day's Office and First Vespers (Evening Prayer I) of the following day be assigned for celebration on the same day, then Vespers (Evening Prayer) of the celebration with the higher rank in the Table of Liturgical Days takes precedence; in cases of equal rank, Vespers (Evening Prayer) of the current day takes precedence.

JANUARY

Cal.	1	The Octave Day of the Nativity of the Lord SOLEMNITY OF MARY, THE HOLY MOTHER OF GOD	Solemnity
IV	2	Sts Basil the Great and Gregory Nazianzen, Bishops and Doctors of the Church	Memorial
III	3	*The Most Holy Name of Jesus**	
Eve	4		
Nones	5		
VIII	6	THE EPIPHANY OF THE LORD	Solemnity
		In England and Wales: On the nearest Sunday between 2nd and 8th January.	
VII	7	*St Raymond of Penyafort, Priest*	
VI	8		
V	9		
IV	10		
III	11		
Eve	12	In England: *St Aelred of Rievaulx*	
Ides	13	*St Hilary, Bishop and Doctor of the Church*	
		In Scotland: St Kentigern, Bishop	Feast
XIX	14		
XVIII	15		
XVII	16		
XVI	17	St Anthony, Abbot	Memorial
XV	18		
XIV	19	In England: *St Wulstan, Bishop*	
XIII	20	*St Fabian, Pope and Martyr* *St Sebastian, Martyr*	
XII	21	St Agnes, Virgin and Martyr	Memorial
XI	22	*St Vincent, Deacon and Martyr*	
X	23		
IX	24	St Francis de Sales, Bishop and Doctor of the Church	Memorial
VIII	25	The Conversion of St Paul the Apostle	Feast
VII	26	Sts Timothy and Titus, Bishops	Memorial
VI	27	*St Angela Merici, Virgin*	
V	28	St Thomas Aquinas, Priest and Doctor of the Church	Memorial
IV	29		
III	30		
Eve	31	St John Bosco, Priest	Memorial

Sunday after 6 January: The Baptism of the Lord   Feast

When the Solemnity of the Epiphany is transferred to the Sunday that occurs on 7th or 8th January, the Feast of the Baptism of the Lord is celebrated on the following Monday.

* When the rank of the celebration is not indicated, it is an Optional Memorial.

FEBRUARY

Cal.	1		
IV	2	THE PRESENTATION OF THE LORD	Feast
III	3	*St Blaise, Bishop and Martyr*	
		St Ansgar, Bishop	
Eve	4		
Nones	5	St Agatha, Virgin and Martyr	Memorial
VIII	6	St Paul Miki and Companions, Martyrs	Memorial
VII	7		
VI	8	*St Jerome Emiliani*	
		St Josephine Bakhita, Virgin	
V	9	In Wales: *St Teilo, Bishop*	
IV	10	St Scholastica, Virgin	Memorial
III	11	*Our Lady of Lourdes*	
Eve	12		
Ides	13		
XVI	14	Sts Cyril, Monk, and Methodius, Bishop	Memorial (In Europe: Feast)
XV	15		
XIV	16		
XIII	17	*The Seven Holy Founders of the Servite Order*	
XII	18		
XI	19		
X	20		
IX	21	*St Peter Damian, Bishop and Doctor of the Church*	
VIII	22	THE CHAIR OF ST PETER THE APOSTLE	Feast
VII	23	St Polycarp, Bishop and Martyr	Memorial
VI	24		
V	25		
IV	26		
III	27		
Eve	28		

173

MARCH

Cal.	1	In Wales: ST DAVID, BISHOP, PATRON OF WALES	Solemnity
		In England: St David, Bishop, Patron of Wales	Feast
VI	2		
V	3		
IV	4	*St Casimir*	
III	5		
Eve	6		
Nones	7	Sts Perpetua and Felicity, Martyrs	Memorial
VIII	8	*St John of God, Religious*	
VII	9	*St Frances of Rome, Religious*	
VI	10	In Scotland: St John Ogilvie, Martyr	Feast
V	11		
IV	12		
III	13		
Eve	14		
Ides	15		
XVII	16		
XVI	17	*St Patrick, Bishop*	
		In England: St Patrick, Bishop, Patron Of Ireland	Feast
		In Scotland: St Patrick, Bishop	Feast
XV	18	*St Cyril of Jerusalem, Bishop and Doctor of the Church*	
XIV	19	ST JOSEPH, SPOUSE OF THE BLESSED VIRGIN MARY	Solemnity
XIII	20		
XII	21		
XI	22		
X	23	*St Turibius of Mogrovejo, Bishop*	
IX	24		
VIII	25	THE ANNUNCIATION OF THE LORD	Solemnity
VII	26		
VI	27		
V	28		
IV	29		
III	30		
Eve	31		

APRIL

Cal.	1		
IV	2	*St Francis of Paola, Hermit*	
III	3		
Eve	4	*St Isidore, Bishop and Doctor of the Church*	
Nones	5	*St Vincent Ferrer, Priest*	
VIII	6		
VII	7	St John Baptist de la Salle, Priest	Memorial
VI	8		
V	9		
IV	10		
III	11	St Stanislaus, Bishop and Martyr	Memorial
Eve	12		
Ides	13	*St Martin I, Pope and Martyr*	
XVIII	14		
XVII	15		
XVI	16		
XV	17		
XIV	18		
XIII	19		
XII	20	In Wales: *St Beuno, Abbot*	
XI	21	*St Anselm, Bishop and Doctor of the Church*	
		In England: *St Anselm, Bishop and Doctor of the Church*	
X	22		
IX	23	*St George, Martyr*	
		St Adalbert, Bishop and Martyr	
		In England: ST GEORGE, MARTYR,	
		PATRON OF ENGLAND	Solemnity
VIII	24	*St Fidelis of Sigmaringen, Priest and Martyr*	
		In England: *St Adalbert, Bishop and Martyr*	
VII	25	ST MARK, EVANGELIST	Feast
VI	26		
V	27		
IV	28	*St Peter Chanel, Priest and Martyr*	
		St Louis Grignion de Montfort, Priest	
III	29	St Catherine of Siena, Virgin and Doctor	
		of the Church	Memorial
			(In Europe: Feast)
Eve	30	*St Pius V, Pope*	

MAY

Cal.	1	*St Joseph the Worker*	
VI	2	St Athanasius, Bishop and Doctor of the Church	Memorial
V	3	STS PHILIP AND JAMES, APOSTLES	Feast
IV	4	In England: THE ENGLISH MARTYRS	Feast
III	5	In Wales: *St Asaph, Bishop*	
Eve	6		
Nones	7		
VIII	8		
VII	9		
VI	10		
V	11		
IV	12	*Sts Nereus and Achilleus, Martyrs*	
		St Pancras, Martyr	
III	13	*Our Lady of Fatima*	
Eve	14	ST MATTHIAS, APOSTLE	Feast
Ides	15		
XVII	16		
XVI	17		
XV	18	*St John I, Pope and Martyr*	
XIV	19	In England: *St Dunstan, Bishop*	
XIII	20	*St Bernardine of Siena, Priest*	
XII	21	*St Christopher Magallanes, Priest, and Companions, Martyrs*	
XI	22	*St Rita of Cascia, Religious*	
X	23		
IX	24		
VIII	25	*St Bede the Venerable, Priest and Doctor of the Church*	
		St Gregory VII, Pope	
		St *Mary Magdalene de' Pazzi, Virgin*	
		In England: St Bede the Venerable, Priest	
		and Doctor of the Church	Memorial
VII	26	St Philip Neri, Priest	Memorial
VI	27	*St Augustine of Canterbury, Bishop*	
		In England: ST AUGUSTINE OF CANTERBURY, BISHOP	Feast
V	28		
IV	29		
III	30		
Eve	31	THE VISITATION OF THE BLESSED VIRGIN MARY	Feast

First Sunday after Pentecost
            THE MOST HOLY TRINITY   Solemnity

Thursday after the Most Holy Trinity
            THE MOST HOLY BODY AND BLOOD OF CHRIST   Solemnity
            In England and Wales: Sunday after the Most Holy Trinity

JUNE

Cal.	1	St Justin, Martyr	Memorial
IV	2	*Sts Marcellinus and Peter, Martyrs*	
III	3	St Charles Lwanga and Companions, Martyrs	Memorial
Eve	4		
Nones	5	St Boniface, Bishop and Martyr	Memorial
		In England: St Boniface, Bishop and Martyr	Memorial
VIII	6	*St Norbert, Bishop*	
VII	7		
VI	8		
V	9	*St Ephrem, Deacon and Doctor of the Church*	
		In Scotland: St Columba, Abbot	Feast
		In England: *St Columba, Abbot*	
IV	10		
III	11	St Barnabas, Apostle	Memorial
Eve	12		
Ides	13	St Anthony of Padua, Priest and Doctor of the Church	Memorial
XVIII	14		
XVII	15		
XVI	16	In England: *St Richard of Chichester, Bishop*	
XV	17		
XIV	18		
XIII	19	*St Romuald, Abbot*	
XII	20	In England: *St Alban, Martyr*	
		In Wales: *Sts Alban, Julius and Aaron, Protomartyrs of Britain*	
XI	21	St Aloysius Gonzaga, Religious	Memorial
X	22	*St Paulinus of Nola, Bishop*	
		Sts John Fisher, Bishop, and Thomas More, Martyrs	
		In England: St John Fisher, Bishop, and Thomas More, Martyrs	Feast
IX	23	In England: *St Etheldreda (Audrey), Virgin*	
VIII	24	THE NATIVITY OF ST JOHN THE BAPTIST	Solemnity
VII	25		
VI	26		
V	27	*St Cyril of Alexandria, Bishop and Doctor of the Church*	
IV	28	St Irenaeus, Bishop and Martyr	Memorial
III	29	STS PETER AND PAUL, APOSTLES	Solemnity
Eve	30	*The First Martyrs of the Holy Roman Church*	

Friday after the Second Sunday after Pentecost		
THE MOST SACRED HEART OF JESUS		Solemnity
Saturday after the Second Sunday after Pentecost		
The Immaculate Heart of the Blessed Virgin Mary		Memorial

JULY

Cal.	1	In England: *St Oliver Plunket, Bishop and Martyr*	
VI	2		
V	3	Sᴛ Tʜᴏᴍᴀs, Aᴘᴏsᴛʟᴇ	Feast
IV	4	*St Elizabeth of Portugal*	
III	5	*St Anthony Zaccaria, Priest*	
Eve	6	*St Maria Goretti, Virgin and Martyr*	
Nones	7		
VIII	8		
VII	9	*St Augustine Zhao Rong, Priest, and Companions, Martyrs*	
		In Scotland: Oᴜʀ Lᴀᴅʏ ᴏғ Aʙᴇʀᴅᴇᴇɴ	Feast
VI	10		
V	11	St Benedict, Abbot	Memorial
			(In Europe: Feast)
IV	12	In Wales: *St John Jones, Priest and Martyr*	
III	13	*St Henry*	
Eve	14	*St Camillus de Lellis, Priest*	
Ides	15	St Bonaventure, Bishop and Doctor	
		of the Church	Memorial
XVII	16	*Our Lady of Mount Carmel*	
XVI	17		
XV	18		
XIV	19		
XIII	20	*St Apollinaris, Bishop and Martyr*	
XII	21	*St Lawrence of Brindisi, Priest and Doctor of the Church*	
XI	22	St Mary Magdalene	Memorial
X	23	*St Bridget, Religious*	(In Europe: Feast)
		In Wales: *Sts Philip Evans and John Lloyd, Priests and Martyrs*	
IX	24	*St Sharbel Makhlūf, Priest*	
VIII	25	Sᴛ Jᴀᴍᴇs, Aᴘᴏsᴛʟᴇ	Feast
VII	26	Sts Joachim and Anne,	
		Parents of the Blessed Virgin Mary	Memorial
VI	27		
V	28		
IV	29	St Martha	Memorial
III	30	*St Peter Chrysologus, Bishop and Doctor of the Church*	
Eve	31	St Ignatius of Loyola, Priest	Memorial

178

AUGUST

Cal.	1	St Alphonsus Mary Liguori, Bishop and Doctor of the Church	Memorial
IV	2	*St Eusebius of Vercelli, Bishop*	
		St Peter Julian Eymard, Priest	
III	3	In Wales: *St Germanus of Auxerre, Bishop*	
Eve	4	St John Mary Vianney, Priest	Memorial
Nones	5	*The Dedication of the Basilica of St Mary Major*	
VIII	6	THE TRANSFIGURATION OF THE LORD	Feast
VII	7	*St Sixtus II, Pope, and Companions, Martyrs*	
		St Cajetan, Priest	
VI	8	St Dominic, Priest	Memorial
V	9	*St Teresa Benedicta of the Cross, Virgin and Martyr*	
			(In Europe: Feast)
IV	10	ST LAWRENCE, DEACON AND MARTYR	Feast
III	11	St Clare, Virgin	Memorial
Eve	12	*St Jane Frances de Chantal, Religious*	
Ides	13	*Sts Pontian, Pope, and Hippolytus, Priest, Martyrs*	
XIX	14	St Maximilian Mary Kolbe, Priest and Martyr	Memorial
XVIII	15	THE ASSUMPTION OF THE BLESSED VIRGIN MARY	Solemnity
XVII	16	*St Stephen of Hungary*	
XVI	17		
XV	18		
XIV	19	*St John Eudes, Priest*	
XIII	20	St Bernard, Abbot and Doctor of the Church	Memorial
XII	21	St Pius X, Pope	Memorial
XI	22	The Queenship of the Blessed Virgin Mary	Memorial
X	23	*St Rose of Lima, Virgin*	
IX	24	ST BARTHOLOMEW, APOSTLE	Feast
VIII	25	*St Louis*	
		St Joseph Calasanz, Priest	
VII	26	In England: *Bl Dominic of the Mother of God, Priest*	
		In Wales: *St David Lewis, Priest and Martyr*	
VI	27	St Monica	Memorial
V	28	St Augustine, Bishop and Doctor of the Church	Memorial
IV	29	The Passion of St John the Baptist	Memorial
III	30	In England: *Sts Margaret Clitherow, Anne Line and Margaret Ward, Martyrs*	
Eve	31	In England: *St Aidan, Bishop, and Saints of Lindisfarne*	

179

SEPTEMBER

Cal.	1		
IV	2		
III	3	St Gregory the Great, Pope and Doctor of the Church	Memorial
		In England: St Gregory the Great, Pope and Doctor of the Church	Feast
Eve	4	In England: *St Cuthbert, Bishop*	
Nones	5		
VIII	6		
VII	7		
VI	8	The Nativity of the Blessed Virgin Mary	Feast
V	9	*St Peter Claver, Priest*	
IV	10		
III	11	In Wales: St Deiniol, Bishop	
Eve	12	*The Most Holy Name of Mary*	
Ides	13	St John Chrysostom, Bishop and Doctor of the Church	Memorial
XVIII	14	The Exaltation of the Holy Cross	Feast
XVII	15	Our Lady of Sorrows	Memorial
XVI	16	Sts Cornelius, Pope, and Cyprian, Bishop, Martyrs	Memorial
		In Scotland: St Ninian, Bishop	Feast
XV	17	*St Robert Bellarmine, Bishop and Doctor of the Church*	
XIV	18		
XIII	19	*St Januarius, Bishop and Martyr*	
		In England: *St Theodore of Canterbury, Bishop*	
XII	20	Sts Andrew Kim Tae-gŏn, Priest, and Paul Chŏng Ha-sang, and Companions, Martyrs	Memorial
XI	21	St Matthew, Apostle and Evangelist	Feast
X	22		
IX	23	St Pius of Pietrelcina, Priest	Memorial
VIII	24	In England: Our Lady of Walsingham	Memorial
VII	25		
VI	26	*Sts Cosmas and Damian, Martyrs*	
V	27	St Vincent de Paul, Priest	Memorial
IV	28	*St Wenceslaus, Martyr*	
		St Lawrence Ruiz and Companions, Martyrs	
III	29	Sts Michael, Gabriel and Raphael, Archangels	Feast
Eve	30	St Jerome, Priest and Doctor of the Church	Memorial

OCTOBER

Cal.	1	St Thérèse of the Child Jesus,	
		Virgin and Doctor of the Church	Memorial
VI	2	The Holy Guardian Angels	Memorial
V	3		
IV	4	St Francis of Assisi	Memorial
III	5		
Eve	6	*St Bruno, Priest*	
Nones	7	Our Lady of the Rosary	Memorial
VIII	8		
VII	9	*St Denis, Bishop, and Companions, Martyrs*	
		St John Leonardi, Priest	
		In England: *Bl John Henry Newman, Priest*	
VI	10	In England: *St Paulinus of York, Bishop*	
V	11		
IV	12	In England: *St Wilfrid, Bishop*	
III	13	In England: *St Edward the Confessor*	
Eve	14	*St Callistus I, Pope and Martyr*	
Ides	15	St Teresa of Jesus, Virgin and Doctor	
		of the Church	Memorial
XVII	16	*St Hedwig, Religious*	
		St Margaret Mary Alacoque, Virgin	
		In Wales: *St Richard Gwyn, Martyr*	
XVI	17	St Ignatius of Antioch, Bishop and Martyr	Memorial
XV	18	Sᴛ Lᴜᴋᴇ, Eᴠᴀɴɢᴇʟɪsᴛ	Feast
XIV	19	*Sts John de Brébeuf and Isaac Jogues, Priests,*	
		and Companions, Martyrs	
		St Paul of the Cross, Priest	
XIII	20		
XII	21		
XI	22		
X	23	*St John of Capistrano, Priest*	
IX	24	*St Anthony Mary Claret, Bishop*	
VIII	25	In Wales: Sɪx Wᴇʟsʜ Mᴀʀᴛʏʀs ᴀɴᴅ ᴛʜᴇɪʀ Cᴏᴍᴘᴀɴɪᴏɴs	Feast
VII	26	In England: *Sts Chad and Cedd, Bishops*	
VI	27		
V	28	Sᴛs Sɪᴍᴏɴ ᴀɴᴅ Jᴜᴅᴇ, Aᴘᴏsᴛʟᴇs	Feast
IV	29		
III	30		
Eve	31		

NOVEMBER

Cal.	1	ALL SAINTS	Solemnity
IV	2	THE COMMEMORATION OF ALL THE FAITHFUL DEPARTED (ALL SOULS DAY)	
III	3	*St Martin de Porres, Religious*	
		In England: *St Winifride, Virgin*	
		In Wales: *St Winifride, Virgin*	
Eve	4	St Charles Borromeo, Bishop	Memorial
Nones	5		
VIII	6	In Wales: *St Illtud, Abbot*	
VII	7	In England: *St Willibrord, Bishop*	
VI	8	In Wales: ALL SAINTS OF WALES	Feast
		In Scotland: Bl John Duns Scotus, Priest	Memorial
V	9	THE DEDICATION OF THE LATERAN BASILICA	Feast
IV	10	St Leo the Great, Pope and Doctor of the Church	Memorial
III	11	St Martin of Tours, Bishop	Memorial
Eve	12	St Josaphat, Bishop and Martyr	Memorial
Ides	13		
XVIII	14	In Wales: *St Dyfrig, Bishop*	
XVII	15	*St Albert the Great, Bishop and Doctor of the Church*	
XVI	16	*St Margaret of Scotland*	
		St Gertrude, Virgin	
		In Scotland: ST MARGARET, SECONDARY PATRON OF SCOTLAND	Feast
		In England: *St Edmund of Abingdon, Bishop*	
XV	17	St Elizabeth of Hungary, Religious	Memorial
			(In England: Optional Memorial)
		In England: *St Hilda, Religious*	
		In England: *St Hugh of Lincoln, Bishop*	
XIV	18	*The Dedication of the Basilicas of Sts Peter and Paul, Apostles*	
XIII	19		
XII	20		
XI	21	The Presentation of the Blessed Virgin Mary	Memorial
X	22	St Cecilia, Virgin and Martyr	Memorial
IX	23	*St Clement I, Pope and Martyr*	
		St Columban, Abbot	
VIII	24	St Andrew Dũng-Lạc, Priest, and Companions, Martyrs	Memorial
VII	25	*St Catherine of Alexandria, Virgin and Martyr*	
VI	26		
V	27		
IV	28		
III	29		
Eve	30	ST ANDREW, APOSTLE	Feast
		In Scotland: ST ANDREW, APOSTLE, PATRON OF SCOTLAND	Solemnity
		In England: ST ANDREW, APOSTLE, PATRON OF SCOTLAND	Feast

Last Sunday in Ordinary Time: OUR LORD JESUS CHRIST, KING OF THE UNIVERSE — Solemnity

DECEMBER

Cal.	1		
IV	2		
III	3	St Francis Xavier, Priest	Memorial
Eve	4	*St John Damascene, Priest and Doctor of the Church*	
Nones	5		
VIII	6	*St Nicholas, Bishop*	
VII	7	St Ambrose, Bishop and Doctor of the Church	Memorial
VI	8	THE IMMACULATE CONCEPTION	
		OF THE BLESSED VIRGIN MARY	Solemnity
V	9	*St Juan Diego Cuauhtlatoatzin*	
IV	10	In Wales: *St John Roberts, Priest and Martyr*	
III	11	*St Damasus I, Pope*	
Eve	12	*Our Lady of Guadalupe*	
Ides	13	St Lucy, Virgin and Martyr	Memorial
XIX	14	St John of the Cross, Priest and Doctor	
		of the Church	Memorial
XVIII	15		
XVII	16		
XVI	17		
XV	18		
XIV	19		
XIII	20		
XII	21	*St Peter Canisius, Priest and Doctor of the Church*	
XI	22		
X	23	*St John of Kanty, Priest*	
IX	24		
VIII	25	THE NATIVITY OF THE LORD (CHRISTMAS)	Solemnity
VII	26	St Stephen, The First Martyr	Feast
VI	27	St John, Apostle and Evangelist	Feast
V	28	The Holy Innocents, Martyrs	Feast
IV	29	*St Thomas Becket, Bishop and Martyr*	
		In England: St Thomas Becket, Bishop and Martyr	
		Patron of Pastoral Clergy in England and Wales	Feast
III	30		
Eve	31	*St Sylvester I, Pope*	

Sunday within the Octave of the Nativity, or, if there is no Sunday, 30 December:

		The Holy Family of Jesus, Mary, and Joseph	Feast